JOURNEY OF ACCEPTANCE

Journey of Acceptance

LIVING AUTISTIC

Sanyub S.

Spectra Enterprise

Contents

Table Of Content

Chapter 1: "In the Spectrum's Embrace"

1.1 Introduction to the diverse world of autism.

1.2 Exploring the spectrum's nuances and dispelling common myths.

1.3 Personal stories illustrating the unique experiences within the autism community.

Chapter 2: "The Family Portrait"

2.1 Examining the pivotal role of families in the journey of acceptance.

2.2 Challenges and triumphs faced by families with autistic members.

2.3 Strategies for fostering acceptance within the family unit.

Chapter 3: "Early Steps: Navigating Childhood"

3.1 Understanding early signs and diagnosis of autism.

3.2 Parenting strategies for nurturing a child on the spectrum.

3.3 The importance of early intervention and inclusive education.

Chapter 4: "Navigating the School Landscape"

4.1 Challenges within the educational system for autistic individuals.

4.2 Successful models of inclusive education.

4.3 Empowering educators to support neurodiverse students.

Chapter 5: "Beyond Labels: Identity and Self-Discovery"

5.1 Personal narratives of individuals on the spectrum.

5.2 Exploring the development of identity and self-advocacy.

5.3 The impact of societal labels and the journey towards self-acceptance.

Chapter 6: "Challenges and Triumphs in Adolescence"

6.1 Navigating the unique challenges of adolescence with autism.
6.2 Social dynamics, peer relationships, and self-esteem.
6.3 Success stories of individuals overcoming obstacles during this stage.

Chapter 7: "Transitioning to Adulthood"

7.1 Challenges and opportunities for individuals with autism entering adulthood.
7.2 Employment, higher education, and independent living.
7.3 Strategies for supporting a successful transition.

Chapter 8: "Workplace Inclusion: Unleashing Potential"

8.1 The role of employers in fostering a neurodiverse workforce.
8.2 Success stories of companies embracing inclusive hiring practices.
8.3 Creating an autism-friendly workplace culture.

Chapter 9: "Community Connections"

9.1 The importance of community support for individuals on the spectrum.
9.2 Grassroots initiatives promoting inclusivity.
9.3 Building bridges between the autism community and society at large.

Introduction

In the unpredictable woven artwork of human experience, the excursion of acknowledgment holds significant importance, rising above cultural standards and enticing us towards grasping, empathy, and solidarity. Inside this mosaic, there exists an extraordinary way cleared by those exploring the immense and various scene of chemical imbalance. The title "Excursion of Acknowledgment: Living Mentally unbalanced" epitomizes the story that unfurls when people with chemical imbalance, their families, and society all in all set out on an extraordinary undertaking of understanding and embracing neurodiversity.

Chemical imbalance, a neurodevelopmental range jumble, shows itself in a bunch of ways, forming the encounters of the people who explore its shapes. From the earliest long periods of young life to the intricacies of adulthood, people on the chemical imbalance range wrestle with a world that might appear to be puzzling, set apart by nuanced challenges and unprecedented qualities. This excursion of acknowledgment isn't just an investigation of the self yet a mutual journey that welcomes society to rethink its standards, shedding predispositions and embracing the **rich embroidered artwork of contrasts that portray the human condition.**

The odyssey starts with the acknowledgment that chemical imbalance isn't a deviation from the standard however an extraordinary indication of neurological variety. It is an affirmation that every person on the range has a particular arrangement of capacities, viewpoints, and possibilities that add to the more extensive human experience. In understanding chemical imbalance, we strip back the layers of misinterpretations and generalizations, uncovering the real quintessence of those living on the range.

Living medically introverted is a story that rises above indicative marks and provokes us to move past simple resistance to veritable acknowledgment. It requires a change in cultural ideal models, provoking us to see neurodiversity not as a lack to be revised but rather as a range to be praised.

The excursion of acknowledgment is an aggregate obligation to encouraging a comprehensive society where people with mental imbalance are esteemed for their extraordinary commitments, and their voices are heard without bending.

Families become vital partners on this campaign, exploring the frequently unfamiliar territory of bringing up a youngster with chemical imbalance. The excursion of acknowledgment starts inside the nuclear family, where guardians, kin, and stretched out family members figure out how to appreciate and uphold the particular characteristics of their medically introverted friends and family. It includes cultivating a climate where acknowledgment isn't restrictive however an intrinsic piece of the familial texture, permitting people on the range to thrive in an environment of affection, understanding, and support.

Nonetheless, the excursion isn't without its difficulties. The cultural scene can be full of hindrances — errors, marks of shame, and foundational obstructions that hinder the full coordination of people with chemical imbalance. The course of acknowledgment calls for destroying these obstructions and building extensions of compassion and incorporation. It includes pushing for available instruction, significant work amazing open doors, and it isn't simply recognized yet celebrated to make spaces where neurodiversity.

The excursion of acknowledgment is certainly not a one-size-fits-all story. It incorporates an expansive range of encounters, mirroring the variety inside the mental imbalance local area itself. Some might cross this way with a steady organization, while others might confront separation and segregation. It is an excursion set apart by strength, fortitude, and the unflinching obligation to reclassify cultural impression of mental imbalance.

As we dive further into the complexities

of living mentally unbalanced, it becomes clear that the excursion is a unique course of self-revelation and development. People on the range foster survival techniques, improve their one of a kind abilities, and cut out a space for themselves in a world that could not necessarily figure out their point of view. The story is one of wins and difficulties, triumphs and misfortunes, all adding to a rich and finished story that is essentially as different as the actual people.

Additionally, the excursion of acknowledgment reaches out past the individual and familial domains to the more extensive local area. Schools, working environments, and public spaces become fields where inclusivity is tried and, preferably, invigorated. Teachers assume a crucial part in establishing conditions that take care of different learning styles, guaranteeing that each understudy, no matter what their neurodiversity, gets the help and facilities they expect to flourish.

Likewise, bosses are given an amazing chance to saddle the special abilities of people on the mental imbalance range. Organizations that hero variety and incorporation perceive that neurodiversity is a resource, encouraging advancement and imagination inside their groups. The excursion of acknowledgment provokes corporate societies to adjust, furnishing a stage where people with chemical imbalance can contribute genuinely to the labor force.

However, acknowledgment isn't an objective; it is a continuous interaction. Society should constantly advance, destroying predispositions, and testing previously established inclinations. It includes encouraging a culture of tuning in and realizing, where the voices of those on the mental imbalance range are recognized as well as effectively searched out. It requires perceiving that variety isn't a block however an impetus for progress and understanding.

All in all, the excursion of acknowledgment is an odyssey that rises above individual encounters to envelop the aggregate story of a general public that is figuring out how to appreciate and celebrate neurodiversity. "Excursion of Acknowledgment: Residing Medically introverted" typifies the pith of this campaign — an excursion set apart by grasping, sympathy, and the aggregate obligation to make an existence where people on the chemical imbalance range can get by as well as really flourish. As we leave on this journey, let us challenge ourselves to rethink acknowledgment, not as a detached resilience, but rather as a unique festival of the wonderfully fluctuated human experience.

Chapter 1

In the Spectrum's Embrace

In the rich embroidery of human experience, the range of mental imbalance unfurls as a complicated and different scene, a huge scope of varieties, shades, and complexities that all in all characterize the neurodiverse local area. "In the Range's Hug" fills in as a fitting beginning stage for the investigation of this diverse excursion, offering a thorough prologue to the subtleties and difficulties that describe the existences of people on the mental imbalance range.

To leave on this odyssey, it is significant to dissipate normal legends and misinterpretations encompassing mental imbalance. The range is definitely not a solid element yet rather a range that traverses many capacities, difficulties, and one of a kind viewpoints. The primary section sets the stage by testing assumptions, empowering perusers to move toward chemical imbalance with a receptive outlook and a readiness to comprehend the different manners by which it shows.

Through a cautious assessment of individual stories, the part portrays the encounters inside the mental imbalance local area. Every story is a demonstration of the versatility, strength, and uniqueness of people on the range. These accounts act as windows into the existences of the individuals who explore a world that may not necessarily comprehend or oblige their unmistakable perspectives and being.

By sharing these encounters, "In the Range's Hug" expects to overcome any barrier among discernment and reality, cultivating compassion and enlightening the rich variety inside the neurodiverse local area.

As the part unfurls, it becomes clear that the range is definitely not an inflexible system yet a liquid and dynamic continuum. The expression "range" itself suggests changeability, and this variety is a wellspring of solidarity instead of a deficiency. Every person on the range has a remarkable arrangement of gifts, abilities, and difficulties, adding to the extravagance of the human experience. Understanding the range requires an eagerness to embrace this variety and value the range as a mosaic of fluctuated encounters as opposed to a straight movement from 'gentle' to 'extreme.'

"In the Range's Hug" likewise highlights the significance of perceiving the job that cultural perspectives play in forming the encounters of people on the range. The disgrace and generalizations related with mental imbalance can make hindrances to acknowledgment and consideration. By tending to these confusions head-on, the section looks to destroy the boundaries that upset the full incorporation of people with chemical imbalance into society. It requires an aggregate change in context, encouraging perusers to see neurodiversity not as a deviation from the standard but rather as a basic and important part of the human condition.

Families, being the essential help structures for people on the range, assume a focal part in the excursion of acknowledgment. The section investigates the elements of families with mentally unbalanced individuals, revealing insight into the difficulties they face and the victories they experience. It digs into the profound and down to earth parts of nurturing a kid on the range, underlining the significance of encouraging a climate of acknowledgment inside the nuclear family. As families figure out how to explore the intricacies of chemical imbalance, they become necessary partners on the excursion of acknowledgment, adding to the more extensive story of understanding and embracing neurodiversity.

The excursion through "In the Range's Hug" is additionally an investigation of youth and the basic job that early mediation plays in forming the direction of people on the range. Perceiving the indications of mental imbalance right off the bat takes into consideration convenient mediations that can fundamentally influence a kid's turn of events. The section digs into the difficulties looked by guardians and parental figures in acquiring precise determinations and suitable help administrations. It highlights the meaning of comprehensive instruction and underlines the requirement for an all encompassing methodology that thinks about the singular qualities and necessities of every youngster.

As people on the range progress into the school years, they experience another arrangement of difficulties inside the school system. "Exploring the School Scene" turns into a vital part in the excursion of acknowledgment, investigating the hindrances that neurodiverse understudies frequently face and introducing fruitful models of comprehensive training. It advocates for teachers to assume a critical part in establishing conditions that take care of different learning styles, guaranteeing that each understudy, paying little mind to neurodiversity, gets the help and facilities expected to flourish scholastically and socially.

"Past Marks: Personality and Self-Revelation" digs into the complex and developing excursion of character for people on the range. Individual accounts enlighten the difficulties and wins of self-revelation, as people wrestle with cultural marks and assumptions. The part stresses the significance of cultivating a self-appreciation support and self-acknowledgment, empowering people on the range to embrace their interesting personality and contribute legitimately to their general surroundings. It challenges the idea that marks ought to characterize people, encouraging society to see the value in the lavishness that accompanies embracing neurodiversity.

Puberty, frequently a turbulent period for anybody, takes on an interesting aspect for people on the range. "Difficulties and Wins in Pre-adulthood" investigates the social elements, peer connections, and confidence gives that might emerge during this phase of life. Examples of overcoming adversity of people conquering deterrents and finding their place inside their networks give motivation and direction to both those on the range and those looking to comprehend and uphold them. The section highlights the significance of encouraging a comprehensive and strong climate that permits neurodiverse young people to explore the difficulties of immaturity with versatility and strength.

Changing to adulthood addresses a urgent stage in the excursion of acknowledgment, set apart by special difficulties and open doors. "Progressing to Adulthood" inspects the pathways accessible to people with chemical imbalance as they enter adulthood, resolving issues like business, advanced education, and autonomous living. It investigates the methodologies and emotionally supportive networks that add to a fruitful progress, underscoring the requirement for continuous local area and familial help during this basic period.

"Work environment Consideration: Releasing Potential" moves the concentration to the job of bosses in cultivating a neurodiverse labor force. The part presents examples of overcoming adversity of organizations that have embraced comprehensive recruiting rehearses and made mental imbalance amicable working environment societies. It advocates for a change in outlook in corporate mentalities toward neurodiversity, perceiving that people on the range bring remarkable gifts and points of view that can add to development and imagination inside the work environment.

The significance of local area support turns into a focal topic in "Local area Associations." The part investigates grassroots drives that advance inclusivity, building spans between the mental imbalance local area and society at large. It features the meaning of collective endeavors in establishing a climate where people on the range can effectively take part, contribute, and feel a feeling of having a place. Through people group associations, the excursion of acknowledgment turns into a common undertaking, encouraging a feeling of solidarity and aggregate liability.

As the book finishes up with "The Always Advancing Excursion," perusers are welcome to think about the powerful idea of the excursion of acknowledgment. The section stresses that acknowledgment isn't an objective however a continuous interaction that requires nonstop exertion and responsibility. It ponders the fate of neurodiversity, taking into account how cultural perspectives might develop and how people on the range can keep on contributing seriously to a world that is turning out to be progressively mindful of the benefit of embracing contrasts.

"In the Range's Hug" fills in as a complete and enlightening prologue to the many-sided excursion of acknowledgment for people living on the mental imbalance range. It challenges cultural standards, scatters fantasies, and urges perusers to move toward neurodiversity with compassion and an open heart. The parts that follow expand upon this establishment, digging further into the different features of the excursion, at last winding around a story that commends the wealth of the human involvement with all its different structures.

1.1 Introduction to the diverse world of autism.

The prologue to the different universe of chemical imbalance is an entryway into an intricate and complex domain that resists oversimplified order. Mental imbalance, formally known as Chemical imbalance Range Problem (ASD), is certainly not a particular substance yet rather a range enveloping a wide scope of neurodevelopmental contrasts. This starting investigation tries to disentangle the complexities of this range, giving an establishment to understanding the remarkable encounters and difficulties looked by people on the mental imbalance range.

At its center, chemical imbalance is described by contrasts in friendly correspondence and conduct. These distinctions manifest in different ways, leading to a range that ranges from the people who might need significant help to the individuals who might display milder difficulties. The expression "range" is conscious in its affirmation of the tremendous variety inside the mental imbalance local area, accentuating that no two people are similar in their show of the problem.

One of the basic perspectives to get a handle on in the different universe of chemical imbalance is the idea of neurodiversity. Neurodiversity challenges the customary clinical model that sees neurological contrasts as shortages to be rectified. All things being equal, it sets that neurological varieties, incorporating those related with mental imbalance, are regular articulations of human variety.

This change in outlook welcomes a rethinking of chemical imbalance from an issue expecting standardization to a one of a kind approach to being that adds to the rich embroidery of human life.

It is fundamental to perceive that chemical imbalance doesn't segregate in light of variables like orientation, race, or financial status. The pervasiveness of chemical imbalance is seen across assorted populaces, featuring the general idea of these neurological contrasts. Notwithstanding, cultural elements can impact the experience of people on the range, with abberations in admittance to assets and backing administrations adding to differing results.

The symptomatic standards for mental imbalance have developed over the long haul, mirroring a more profound comprehension of the range's complexities. The Demonstrative and Measurable Manual of Mental Problems (DSM-5), a generally involved order framework for mental issues, presented the expression "Chemical imbalance Range Issue" in 2013. This shift merged a few beforehand particular judgments, (for example, Asperger's condition and unavoidable formative problem not in any case determined) under a solitary umbrella, stressing the continuum of mentally unbalanced characteristics.

As we explore the different universe of chemical imbalance, it is essential to scatter normal fantasies and misinterpretations that have sustained shame and misjudging. Chemical imbalance isn't a consequence of poor nurturing or an absence of discipline; it is a neurological distinction with an intricate exchange of hereditary and ecological elements. The basic excursion into the universe of mental imbalance challenges assumptions, cultivating a more precise and compassionate comprehension of this different range.

Besides, the assorted universe of mental imbalance reaches out past the person to incorporate families, instructors, and society at large. Families assume a focal part in the existences of people on the range, frequently going about as promoters and emotionally supportive networks. Instructors bear the obligation of establishing comprehensive conditions that take care of assorted learning styles, guaranteeing that neurodiverse understudies get the vital facilities to flourish scholastically and socially.

Society's impression of chemical imbalance fundamentally impacts the encounters of people on the range. Marks of shame and generalizations can make obstructions to acknowledgment and incorporation, blocking the full combination of neurodiverse people into different aspects of society. The different universe of mental imbalance, in this way, requires an aggregate change in cultural perspectives — a development from simple resilience to certifiable acknowledgment.

Inside the range, there are shared traits, yet there are additionally immense contrasts in how mental imbalance shows. A few people might encounter difficulties in friendly correspondence, like troubles with nonverbal prompts or keeping up with proportional discussions. Others might show redundant ways of behaving or extreme interests in unambiguous points.

Tangible responsive qualities, where certain boosts might be overpowering, are additionally normal among people on the range.

The different universe of mental imbalance envelops a scope of qualities and gifts. Numerous people with mental imbalance have extraordinary abilities, for example, outstanding memory, tender loving care, or an uplifted capacity to zero in on unambiguous undertakings. These qualities can be outfit and praised, adding to the comprehension that neurodiversity isn't just about difficulties yet in addition about the lavishness of special points of view and capacities.

In digging into the different universe of mental imbalance, it is essential to perceive that every person on the range is an independent being with their own story. Individual stories offer powerful looks into the existences of those exploring the range, giving a refining contact to the clinical depictions of the issue. These stories enlighten the victories, challenges, and ordinary encounters of people on the range, separating boundaries and cultivating compassion.

The prologue to the different universe of chemical imbalance makes way for a more significant investigation of the complexities that continue in ensuing sections. It fills in as an establishment for the excursion of acknowledgment, encouraging perusers to move toward chemical imbalance with interest, transparency, and an eagerness to embrace the variety that portrays the neurodiverse local area. As the story unfurls, it welcomes perusers to reevaluate their discernments, challenge generalizations, and effectively partake in making a more comprehensive and grasping society for people on the chemical imbalance range.

1.2 Exploring the spectrum's nuances and dispelling common myths.

Investigating the subtleties of the chemical imbalance range includes digging into the bunch manners by which Chemical imbalance Range Issue (ASD) shows, perceiving the variety of encounters that people on the range experience. The range is definitely not a direct movement from 'gentle' to 'extreme' yet rather an intricate continuum, incorporating a huge swath of qualities, difficulties, and novel attributes.

One of the essential subtleties inside the range lies in the changeability of social correspondence and communication. While certain people with chemical imbalance might confront hardships in understanding and answering meaningful gestures, others might show social ways of behaving that adjust all the more intimately with average turn of events. The range's subtleties challenge the ordinary comprehension of social communications, encouraging us to embrace a more extensive point of view that obliges different approaches to interfacing with others.

One more feature of the range's subtleties is the fluctuation in conduct and interests. Dull ways of behaving, a typical trait of mental imbalance, can appear in changed structures, going from generalized developments to extreme distractions with explicit themes or items. A few people might show unbending schedules, tracking down solace in consistency, while others might have a more adaptable way to deal with day to day exercises. Investigating these subtleties supports a nuanced comprehension of the range, perceiving that what might be really difficult for one individual could be a wellspring of euphoria or solace for another.

Tangible responsive qualities address one more layer of intricacy inside the range. People on the mental imbalance range might encounter uplifted or lessened aversion to tactile improvements, like lights, sounds, surfaces, or scents. These awarenesses can fundamentally affect day to day existence, impacting inclinations for specific conditions and exercises. By investigating these tangible subtleties, we gain understanding into the tactile variety that describes the encounters of people on the range.

Dispersing normal fantasies encompassing chemical imbalance is a fundamental piece of the investigation of the range's subtleties. Legends frequently propagate misconstruing and add to the shame related with mental imbalance. One predominant legend is the idea that people with chemical imbalance need compassion. As a general rule, individuals on the range might insight and express compassion in special ways, testing conventional assumptions. By scattering this fantasy, we make the way for a more precise comprehension of the profound existences of people with chemical imbalance.

Another normal fantasy is the conviction that all people with chemical imbalance have unprecedented academic capacities. While certain people on the range may to be sure have remarkable abilities or gifts, perceiving the variety of capacities inside the mental imbalance community is pivotal. The range's subtleties stretch out past generalizations, recognizing that every individual is exceptional and complex in their assets and difficulties.

The legend of a one-size-fits-all way to deal with chemical imbalance is likewise dissipated while investigating the range's subtleties. The possibility that mediations or facilities that work for one individual will be all around powerful neglects the individualized idea of chemical imbalance. Fitting help to the particular requirements of every individual on the range is fundamental for cultivating achievement and prosperity. Perceiving and regarding these distinctions is basic to advancing inclusivity and understanding.

Dispersing fantasies likewise includes testing the off track idea that mental imbalance is a consequence of careless nurturing or ecological elements. Chemical imbalance has areas of strength for a part, and keeping in mind that ecological elements might assume a part, they don't suggest shortcoming with respect to guardians. Understanding the organic premise of chemical imbalance disperses fault and cultivates compassion for families exploring the difficulties related with the range.

Investigating the range's subtleties and dispersing normal legends requires a change in context — an eagerness to embrace intricacy, reject distorted stories, and perceive the intrinsic variety inside the chemical imbalance range. The excursion of scattering fantasies is a continuous cycle that includes schooling, mindfulness, and support to challenge misinterpretations and advance a more exact comprehension of mental imbalance.

As we investigate these subtleties, it becomes clear that the range is definitely not a static or unbending build. It is a dynamic and developing scene molded by the connections among hereditary and natural variables. The intricacy of the range provokes us to move past assumptions and participate in a ceaseless course of learning and forgetting.

As well as dissipating fantasies, it is fundamental to recognize that people on the chemical imbalance range may likewise confront co-happening conditions, like nervousness, sorrow, or consideration shortage/hyperactivity jumble (ADHD). The multifacetedness of these circumstances further highlights the significance of a comprehensive and individualized way to deal with understanding and supporting people on the range. Investigating these crossing points adds to a more thorough and nuanced comprehension of the difficulties and qualities related with chemical imbalance.

Besides, the range's subtleties reach out past the person to include the interconnection of orientation, race, and social variables. By and large, research and demonstrative models have been overwhelmingly founded on the encounters of white guys, prompting a likely underrepresentation of different voices inside the chemical imbalance local area. Perceiving and tending to these differences is crucial for guaranteeing that how we might interpret the range is comprehensive and intelligent of the different encounters, everything being equal, no matter what their experience.

The excursion of investigating the range's subtleties isn't just about scattering fantasies yet in addition about encouraging compassion and advancing acknowledgment. By recognizing the extravagance of variety inside the chemical imbalance local area, we make an establishment for building comprehensive and steady networks. This investigation provokes us to move past a deficiency based model of survey chemical imbalance and on second thought value the special viewpoints and commitments that people on the range bring to the world.

Besides, the investigation of the range's subtleties welcomes us to scrutinize the idea of "predictability" itself. What is viewed as ordinary or regular is many times a social build that can reject and underestimate the people who fall outside customary assumptions. Embracing the range's variety challenges the thought of a solitary, regulating approach to being and energizes an additional comprehensive and sympathetic viewpoint that values neurodiversity as a necessary piece of the human experience.

All in all, investigating the subtleties of the mental imbalance range and dispersing normal legends is a complex excursion that includes recognizing and embracing variety. It requires a guarantee to continuous schooling, mindfulness, and support to challenge misguided judgments and advance a more exact comprehension of mental imbalance. By exploring this intricate territory with receptiveness and compassion, we add to the formation of a world that qualities and commends the novel qualities and points of view of people on the range.

1.3 Personal stories illustrating the unique experiences within the autism community.

Individual stories act as windows into the rich and shifted encounters inside the mental imbalance local area, offering novel viewpoints that challenge generalizations and give knowledge into the different existences of people on the range. These stories not just refine the clinical portrayals of Chemical imbalance Range Problem (ASD) yet in addition cultivate sympathy, understanding, and a more profound association between people with chemical imbalance and the more extensive local area.

Every individual story is an embroidery woven with the strings of individual qualities, difficulties, wins, and snapshots of significant knowledge. Through these accounts, we gain a firsthand comprehension of the remarkable manners by which mental imbalance shows and how it shapes the existences of those exploring the range. While every story is unmistakable, by and large they add to a mosaic that mirrors the intricacy and variety of the mental imbalance local area.

One convincing part of individual stories inside the mental imbalance local area is the manner by which people articulate their encounters of social connection. For some's purposes, exploring social subtleties can be much the same as translating a perplexing code, where nonverbal prompts, signals, and implicit social standards present consistent difficulties. These accounts shed light on the work and mental burden expected to explore social circumstances that might appear to be natural to neurotypical people. They feature the significance of perceiving and esteeming different correspondence styles, testing the idea that there is a generally 'right' method for connecting socially.

Past the difficulties, individual stories frequently enlighten the one of a kind qualities and gifts that people with chemical imbalance offer of real value. A few stories uncover uncommon capacities in regions like math, music, workmanship, or memory review. These gifts challenge assumptions about the limits of people on the range, displaying the lavishness and variety of mental capacities inside the chemical imbalance local area. Individual stories become a festival of these exceptional qualities, encouraging society to move past shortfall based viewpoints and embrace the complex gifts of people with chemical imbalance.

The accounts inside the mental imbalance local area likewise shed light on the tangible encounters that can significantly influence day to day existence. Tactile responsive qualities, whether excessive touchiness or hyposensitivity, are normal among people on the range. Individual stories give looks into a reality where apparently normal tactile boosts — like the murmur of bright lights, the surface of dress, or the flavor of specific food sources — can evoke extreme and in some cases overpowering reactions. These accounts highlight the significance of establishing conditions that oblige tangible variety, supporting for inclusivity in spaces where tactile contrasts might affect solace and prosperity.

Exploring training turns into a focal subject in numerous individual stories inside the mental imbalance local area. The change from youth to formal tutoring presents an extraordinary arrangement of difficulties, going from troubles with tactile over-burden in clamoring conditions to the requirement for individualized learning draws near. Individual stories frequently feature the basic job that steady teachers play in molding positive instructive encounters for people on the range. These accounts advocate for comprehensive schooling that perceives and obliges different learning styles, cultivating a climate where each understudy, paying little heed to neurodiversity, can flourish.

Pre-adulthood, with its inborn social intricacies and assumptions, unfurls contrastingly for people on the range. Individual stories during this phase of life frequently uncover the complexities of shaping fellowships, exploring close connections, and fostering a feeling of personality. Difficulties like social disengagement, tormenting, and the craving for acknowledgment become focal subjects. These stories give important experiences into the close to home scene of puberty with chemical imbalance, underlining the requirement for figuring out, sympathy, and comprehensive social conditions.

Changing to adulthood denotes a critical stage in the individual stories inside the chemical imbalance local area. As people on the range approach freedom, they experience various difficulties connected with work, advanced education, and autonomous living. Individual stories shed light on the boundaries to section into the labor force, the significance of obliging working environment conditions, and the quest for significant and satisfying professions. These stories point out the requirement for cultural changes in perspectives toward neurodiversity, pushing for comprehensive practices that permit people with chemical imbalance to contribute definitively to different areas.

Families assume a critical part in the individual stories inside the chemical imbalance local area. Guardians, kin, and more distant family individuals frequently highlight noticeably as partners and backers. These stories investigate the intricacies of nurturing a youngster with chemical imbalance, the delights, and difficulties of kin connections, and the fundamental job of familial help in the excursion of acknowledgment. Individual stories inside the family setting feature the strength and assurance expected to explore a general public that may not necessarily in every case completely comprehend or oblige neurodiversity.

Also, individual stories inside the mental imbalance local area frequently address the close to home parts of self-revelation and personality. People on the range set out on an excursion to comprehend and embrace their one of a kind selves. These accounts dive into the course of self-acknowledgment, testing cultural assumptions and standards. Individual stories become a useful asset for supporting for self-promotion, independence, and the festival of different personalities inside the chemical imbalance local area.

The multifacetedness of individual stories inside the mental imbalance local area is likewise a basic aspect. The encounters of people with mental imbalance are molded by their neurodiversity as well as by variables like orientation, race, and social foundation. Individual stories that investigate this diversity add to a more nuanced comprehension of how different parts of personality cross and impact each other. These accounts underscore the significance of perceiving and tending to incongruities inside the chemical imbalance local area, upholding for inclusivity that recognizes and regards assorted voices.

Supporting inclusivity and dissipating fantasies is an ongoing idea woven through numerous individual stories inside the chemical imbalance local area. These stories challenge generalizations, face marks of disgrace, and effectively take part in support to make a really understanding and tolerating society. Individual stories become an impetus for more extensive social change, inciting discussions that stretch out past the singular level to impact strategies, organizations, and public discernments.

Taking everything into account, individual stories inside the mental imbalance local area act as strong tributes that enlighten the different and nuanced encounters of people on the range. These stories rise above clinical portrayals and insights, offering a profoundly human viewpoint that cultivates sympathy, understanding, and association. The extravagance of individual stories provokes us to move past generalizations, celebrate variety, and effectively add to a world that hugs and values the one of a kind commitments of people with chemical imbalance.

Chapter 2

The Family Portrait

The relational peculiarity becomes the dominant focal point in the story of mental imbalance, framing a perplexing and cozy scenery against which the special encounters of people on the range unfurl. "The Family Representation" catches the mind boggling transaction of adoration, difficulties, and strength as families explore the strange territory of bringing up a youngster with Mental imbalance Range Issue (ASD). Inside this system, individual stories arise as energetic brushstrokes that paint a powerful and complex family picture.

At the core of "The Family Picture" lies the significant effect of a mental imbalance determination on guardians and kin. The underlying disclosure frequently denotes an essential second, setting off a range of feelings going from disarray and dread to a wild assurance to help and comprehend. The story investigates the close to home excursion of guardians wrestling with the intricacies of mental imbalance, standing up to vulnerabilities about the future, and changing their assumptions and desires.

Kin, as well, assume fundamental parts inside "The Family Representation." Their encounters are particularly molded by the presence of a sibling or sister on the range. The account dives into the intricacies of kin connections, where love coincides with difficulties like the requirement for grasping, the craving for consideration, and the route of cultural discernments. The narratives of kin inside "The Family Picture" feature the strength and flexibility expected to explore a scene that might be both fulfilling and requesting.

In addition, the family picture grows to envelop expanded family members, whose discernments and backing fundamentally impact the familial excursion with mental imbalance. Grandparents, aunties, uncles, and cousins might assume assorted parts, going from backers and partners to wellsprings of extra help or expected misconceptions. These connections mesh into the more extensive embroidery of relational peculiarities, adding to the nuanced representation of a family exploring the range.

"The Family Picture" isn't static yet advances over the long run, reflecting the formative direction of the person with mental imbalance. Youth turns into a basic crossroads, set apart by the quest for a precise finding, mediations, and the progressive acknowledgment of the interesting requirements and qualities of the youngster on the range. The account unfurls as families explore the maze of treatments, instruction plans, and the mission for assets to offer the most ideal help for their youngster.

Schooling turns into a focal subject inside "The Family Picture." The excursion through the schooling system presents novel difficulties, from upholding for comprehensive conditions to tending to individualized advancing requirements. The story investigates the job of guardians as supporters, teachers as partners, and the effect of comprehensive instructive settings on the general prosperity and advancement of the kid on the range. These accounts underscore the significance of cooperative endeavors among families and instructors to establish conditions that cultivate development, understanding, and acknowledgment.

Kin, in their jobs as the two observers and dynamic members in the instructive excursion, explore their own ways inside "The Family Representation." The elements of kin connections are molded by shared encounters, novel difficulties, and the bonds framed through common comprehension and backing. Individual stories inside this story enlighten the strength and empathy that kin bring to the nuclear family, adding to the general flexibility of the familial dynamic.

As the family picture stretches out into pre-adulthood, the account wrestles with the intricacies of social cooperations, freedom, and the quest for individual character. Youthfulness is a period set apart by significant changes, and people on the range might confront remarkable difficulties in exploring the social scene. The family account unfurls as guardians and kin acclimate to the advancing requirements of their young adult relative, investigating techniques for encouraging autonomy, supporting social turn of events, and tending to the close to home subtleties of immaturity with chemical imbalance.

Progressing to adulthood turns into a huge part inside "The Family Picture." The story investigates the difficulties and wins of people with chemical imbalance as they explore the intricacies of adulthood, from business and advanced education to free living. Families become fundamental mainstays of help during this progress, pushing for comprehensive open doors, and attempting to guarantee that their friends and family can lead satisfying and significant lives. The accounts inside this section underscore the continuous responsibility of families to the prosperity and independence of their grown-up relatives on the range.

"The Family Representation" isn't without its snapshots of festivity and satisfaction. Individual stories inside this story catch the victories — both of all shapes and sizes — of people with mental imbalance. From scholarly accomplishments and achievements in friendly collaborations to snapshots of self-articulation and imagination, these accounts portray a family joined in their common triumphs. The story turns into a demonstration of the flexibility and assurance that characterize the familial excursion with chemical imbalance.

However, the difficulties inside "The Family Representation" ought not be put into words. The close to home cost, the promotion exhaustion, and the cultural errors that families face are fundamental parts of the account. The tales inside this representation feature the requirement for encouraging groups of people, both inside the family and in the more extensive local area. They highlight the significance of cultivating grasping, sympathy, and comprehensive practices to mitigate the weights that families might carry on their excursion with chemical imbalance.

The family picture likewise catches the diversity of chemical imbalance with different parts of character. The encounters of families are affected by elements like orientation, race, financial status, and social foundation. Individual stories inside this story add to a more nuanced comprehension of how different convergences shape the familial experience of mental imbalance, underlining the requirement for inclusivity that regards and recognizes different viewpoints.

"The Family Picture" isn't static; it keeps on developing as people with mental imbalance age and as cultural perspectives toward neurodiversity shift. The accounts inside this powerful picture accentuate the significance of continuous promotion, training, and local area commitment. Families become dynamic members in the more extensive development for acknowledgment, consideration, and understanding, reshaping the cultural scene for people in the future of people on the range.

All in all, "The Family Representation" is a story that rises above the clinical depictions of chemical imbalance, offering a profoundly private and human point of view on the familial excursion. It is a story set apart by affection, strength, and the quest for understanding. Individual stories inside this representation add to a more extensive cultural exchange, testing generalizations, scattering fantasies, and pushing for a more caring and comprehensive world for people and families living with chemical imbalance.

2.1 Examining the pivotal role of families in the journey of acceptance.

Looking at the urgent job of families in the excursion of acknowledgment inside the domain of Mental imbalance Range Issue (ASD) uncovers a diverse story of adoration, support, versatility, and development.

Families become focal characters in this story, assuming essential parts in supporting people on the range, testing cultural standards, and advocating acknowledgment. The investigation of this crucial job unfurls as an embroidery woven with the strings of shared encounters, difficulties, and wins inside the familial excursion with mental imbalance.

At the core of the familial excursion lies the snapshot of finding. This urgent second denotes the start of a groundbreaking interaction for families, setting off a scope of feelings from disarray and despondency to an assurance to comprehend and uphold their cherished one. The story investigates the underlying effect of the finding on guardians and kin, revealing insight into the intricacies of grappling with a mental imbalance determination and the ensuing transformation to a new and exceptional relational peculiarity.

The excursion of acknowledgment inside families unfurls as guardians become furious backers for their youngsters on the range. Exploring the intricacies of the medical services framework, instructive foundations, and cultural perspectives requires strength and assurance. Families end up at the front of testing generalizations, pushing for comprehensive practices, and working vigorously to guarantee that their friends and family get the help and facilities expected to flourish. The story stresses the critical job of families as promoters, for their singular individuals as well as for the more extensive mental imbalance local area.

Also, kin inside the familial scene assume essential parts in the excursion of acknowledgment. Their encounters are molded by shared young lives, novel difficulties, and the development of bonds that reach out past the customary kin dynamic. Kin become partners, supporters, and wellsprings of figuring out inside the familial excursion with mental imbalance. The story investigates the effect of growing up with a sibling or sister on the range, featuring the one of a kind viewpoints and qualities that kin offer of real value.

The excursion of acknowledgment reaches out past the close family to incorporate the more extensive organization of family members. Grandparents, aunties, uncles, and cousins become vital pieces of the familial emotionally supportive network. Their jobs fluctuate, going from wellsprings of extra help and understanding to expected wellsprings of misconception or misalignment. The story inspects the effect of more distant family elements on the acknowledgment venture, stressing the significance of encouraging an aggregate comprehension and comprehensive climate inside the bigger nuclear family.

Youth turns into a basic section in the excursion of acknowledgment inside families. The account investigates the quest for an exact finding, the commencement of early mediations, and the slow acknowledgment of the exceptional necessities and qualities of the youngster on the range. Families explore the complexities of treatments, instructive plans, and the mission for assets that can offer the most ideal help for their youngsters. The early years become a developmental period for families, molding their viewpoints, needs, and ways to deal with acknowledgment.

Instruction turns into a focal subject inside the familial excursion of acknowledgment. Guardians frequently end up at the very front of pushing for comprehensive instructive conditions that perceive and oblige the different learning styles of people on the range. The story investigates the difficulties families face in getting proper instructive help, cultivating cooperation with teachers, and establishing conditions that work with the scholar and social improvement of their youngsters. The vital job of families as promoters inside instructive settings turns into a main impetus in the excursion of acknowledgment.

Kin, as witnesses and dynamic members in the instructive excursion, explore their own ways inside the familial scene. The account digs into the intricacies of kin connections inside the instructive setting, investigating the elements of shared encounters, common help, and the extraordinary difficulties that might emerge. Kin become partners chasing after comprehensive training, supporting for their sibling or sister and adding to the familial obligation to acknowledgment inside instructive settings.

Immaturity denotes a critical section inside the familial excursion of acknowledgment. The account investigates the intricacies of social connections, autonomy, and the quest for individual character during this groundbreaking period. Families conform to the advancing requirements of their juvenile relatives, investigating techniques for encouraging freedom, supporting social turn of events, and tending to the profound subtleties of pre-adulthood with mental imbalance. The story features the strength of families as they explore the difficulties and wins of this basic stage inside the excursion of acknowledgment.

Progressing to adulthood turns into an impactful part inside the familial excursion. The account inspects the difficulties and potential open doors looked by people with mental imbalance as they explore the intricacies of adulthood, from work and advanced education to autonomous living. Families become fundamental mainstays of help during this change, supporting for comprehensive open doors and attempting to guarantee that their friends and family can lead satisfying and significant lives. The tales inside this section accentuate the continuous responsibility of families to the prosperity and independence of their grown-up relatives on the range.

The close to home scene inside families turns into a focal subject in the excursion of acknowledgment. The story investigates the delights, disappointments, and snapshots of festivity that accentuate the familial experience of living with mental imbalance. Individual stories inside this scene catch the flexibility and assurance that characterize the familial excursion, underlining the adoration and acknowledgment that tight spot families together. The close to home subtleties inside families become a strong demonstration of the strength and responsibility expected to explore the intricacies of chemical imbalance.

Also, the excursion of acknowledgment inside families is profoundly interlaced with the more extensive cultural setting. Families frequently wind up testing cultural standards, dissipating legends, and effectively captivating in promotion to make an additional comprehensive and grasping world. The account investigates the multifacetedness of familial encounters with cultural perspectives, revealing insight into the manners by which families become influencers inside the more extensive scene of chemical imbalance acknowledgment.

The diversity of the familial excursion likewise reaches out to contemplations of orientation, race, financial status, and social foundation. The story looks at how these converging factors shape the encounters of families inside the excursion of acknowledgment, underlining the requirement for inclusivity that regards and recognizes different viewpoints. The tales inside this story add to a more nuanced comprehension of the manners by which different parts of personality meet and impact the familial experience of chemical imbalance.

"The Urgent Job of Families in the Excursion of Acknowledgment" isn't just a static account yet a developing story. Families effectively add to molding the cultural scene for people in the future of people on the range. The account highlights the significance of progressing support, instruction, and local area commitment to encourage figuring out, compassion, and inclusivity. Families become impetuses for social change, testing generalizations, and effectively taking part in the more extensive development for acknowledgment inside the chemical imbalance local area and then some.

All in all, the investigation of the urgent job of families in the excursion of acknowledgment inside the domain of chemical imbalance divulges a story rich with intricacy, love, and strength. Families arise as focal figures, exploring the difficulties and wins of living with mental imbalance while effectively adding to cultural changes in perspectives. The story underlines the continuous responsibility of families to acknowledgment, understanding, and inclusivity, highlighting their extraordinary job in molding the scene for people on the range and encouraging a more sympathetic and embracing world.

2.2 Challenges and triumphs faced by families with autistic members.

The excursion of families with mentally unbalanced individuals is a story that unfurls with an embroidery of difficulties and wins, laying out a picture of strength, love, and nonstop transformation. Families wind up exploring a perplexing scene set apart by interesting obstacles and surprising triumphs, and the interchange of these components shapes the significant and developing story of existence with chemical imbalance.

One of the essential difficulties looked by families with medically introverted individuals bases on the underlying conclusion. The snapshot of disclosure is in many cases set apart by a combination of feelings, going from shock and forswearing to sorrow and vulnerability about what's in store. Exploring the symptomatic interaction turns into an imposing undertaking, with families catching to fathom how a chemical imbalance conclusion affects their cherished one and for the nuclear family all in all. The excursion of acknowledgment starts here, as families stand up to the truth of chemical imbalance and set out on a way that requests flexibility and strength.

Admittance to suitable assets and backing administrations arises as quite difficult for families with medically introverted individuals. From instructive mediations to helpful projects, families frequently end up in a maze of perplexing frameworks, each with its own arrangement of prerequisites and impediments. Getting the essential help turns into an excursion in itself, requesting time, exertion, and support abilities. The victories, in this unique circumstance, lie in the strength of families who explore administrative labyrinths to guarantee that their friends and family get the most ideal consideration and backing.

Schooling turns into a focal field where families wrestle with the two difficulties and wins. In standard instructive settings, mentally unbalanced people might experience conditions that battle to oblige their remarkable learning styles. Challenges emerge in pushing for comprehensive works on, grasping the individualized necessities of their kid, and cultivating a climate that supports as opposed to ruins scholarly turn of events. Wins arise when families effectively team up with teachers to make comprehensive spaces, guaranteeing that their friends and family can flourish scholastically and socially.

Kin inside these families face an unmistakable arrangement of difficulties and wins. The elements of growing up with a mentally unbalanced sibling or sister include a fragile equilibrium of figuring out, compassion, and, on occasion, the requirement for individual consideration. Kin might wind up exploring cultural discernments, defying the real factors of expected social separation, and filling in as supporters for their mentally unbalanced relatives. The victories, in this specific situation, are the bonds fashioned through shared encounters, the advancement of empathy, and the remarkable qualities that kin bring to the familial embroidered artwork.

Pre-adulthood presents another arrangement of intricacies for families with mentally unbalanced individuals. The difficulties rotate around the many-sided social scene of youth, where cultural standards and assumptions might conflict with the novel social elements related with chemical imbalance. Exploring companionships, heartfelt connections, and self-character turns into a territory set apart by the two obstacles and wins. Families witness the flexibility of their friends and family as they explore the intricacies of immaturity, encouraging a feeling of acknowledgment, self-disclosure, and strengthening.

Progressing to adulthood denotes a critical part in the excursion of families with mentally unbalanced individuals. The difficulties envelop business amazing open doors, free living, and the more extensive cultural mentalities towards neurodiversity. Families might wind up wrestling with the restricted accessibility of reasonable business choices and lodging courses of action that take care of the exceptional necessities of their grown-up relatives. The victories inside this domain lie in the assurance of families to advocate for comprehensive practices, challenge generalizations, and set out open doors that permit their friends and family to lead satisfying and significant lives as free grown-ups.

The profound scene of families with mentally unbalanced individuals is both testing and victorious. Personal difficulties might emerge from cultural errors, the continuous promotion weakness, and the heaviness of cultural assumptions. The victories manifest in the adoration that tough situations families together, the festival of exceptional qualities, and the common triumphs, whether enormous or little. Families become versatile mainstays of help, developing a climate that values neurodiversity and difficulties cultural standards.

Besides, the excursion isn't without its monetary difficulties. The expense of treatments, instructive help, and different intercessions can put a critical weight on families. Monetary requirements might restrict admittance to specific assets, making a steady pressure between the longing to offer the most ideal help and the useful real factors of monetary limits. Wins inside this setting are set apart by the creativity and assurance of families to search out elective roads and encouraging groups of people that mitigate monetary strains.

The disgrace related with mental imbalance stays an unavoidable test for families. Cultural misinterpretations and generalizations can prompt a feeling of seclusion and an absence of understanding from the more extensive local area. Families end up effectively participated in testing these marks of shame, advancing mindfulness, and supporting for a more comprehensive and compassionate society. Wins in this space come from the steady destroying of generalizations, the rising consciousness of neurodiversity, and the encouraging of networks that celebrate contrasts.

Emergency minutes, like implosions or tangible over-burden, present exceptional difficulties for families with medically introverted individuals. The unconventionality of these circumstances can be genuinely depleting and socially separating. Families should explore these difficulties with effortlessness and understanding, tracking down ways of supporting their friends and family while likewise dealing with the possible effect on relational intricacies. Wins arise as versatility, as families figure out how to answer with persistence, compassion, and a profound comprehension of their relative's one of a kind necessities.

The multifacetedness of difficulties looked by families with mentally unbalanced individuals becomes clear while considering variables like race, orientation, and financial status. Minimized people group might experience extra boundaries in getting to assets and backing administrations.

The victories inside this setting emerge from the support endeavors that look to address variations, advance inclusivity, and guarantee that all families, paying little mind to foundation, get the help they need.

While challenges persevere, families with mentally unbalanced individuals track down strength in the triumphs, both of all shapes and sizes. The victories arise as promotion achievements, instructive accomplishments, snapshots of association and understanding, and the general flexibility of the nuclear family. The excursion turns into a demonstration of the unfaltering responsibility of families to the acknowledgment, prosperity, and strengthening of their friends and family on the range.

All in all, the excursion of families with mentally unbalanced individuals is a nuanced story set apart by a range of difficulties and wins. It is an account of flexibility, backing, and love, as families explore the intricacies of existence with mental imbalance. The victories arise from beating obstacles as well as from the significant snapshots of association, understanding, and shared triumphs. As society keeps on developing towards more noteworthy acknowledgment and inclusivity, the victories of families with mentally unbalanced individuals add to a more extensive story that praises neurodiversity and backers for an existence where people on the range can thrive and be embraced for what their identity is.

2.3 Strategies for fostering acceptance within the family unit.

Encouraging acknowledgment inside the nuclear family when a part has Chemical imbalance Range Problem (ASD) is an extraordinary excursion set apart by sympathy, understanding, and a pledge to embracing neurodiversity. As families explore this way, they find a horde of methodologies that add to a climate where acknowledgment prospers, making a space where every relative, paying little heed to neurodiversity, is esteemed and perceived.

Correspondence lies at the core of cultivating acknowledgment inside the nuclear family. Transparent discourse permits relatives to share their considerations, feelings, and encounters, encouraging a climate of understanding. Empowering a culture where everybody feels appreciated and recognized destroys expected hindrances to acknowledgment. Correspondence techniques might incorporate customary family gatherings, making a place of refuge for open discussions, and effectively paying attention to every relative's viewpoint.

Training turns into an integral asset in encouraging acknowledgment inside the family. Giving data about mental imbalance, its qualities, and the different ways it shows assists relatives with fostering a more profound comprehension. Instructive systems might include sharing assets, going to studios or care groups, and taking part in conversations that disperse legends and misinterpretations. By outfitting themselves with information, families can explore the difficulties and wins of living with mental imbalance all the more successfully.

Advancing compassion inside the nuclear family is a significant procedure for cultivating acknowledgment. Empowering relatives to place themselves in the shoes of their mentally unbalanced relative forms a groundwork of sympathy and understanding. Exercises, for example, taking part in context taking activities, perusing writing composed by people with mental imbalance, or partaking in compassion building activities can upgrade the family's capacity to feel for the special encounters of their medically introverted part.

Establishing a comprehensive family climate includes adjusting schedules and exercises to oblige the necessities, everything being equal. Perceiving and regarding the tangible responsive qualities and inclinations of the person with chemical imbalance is vital. This might include making changes in accordance with the actual climate, taking into account tactile cordial spaces, and consolidating exercises that take care of assorted interests. Comprehensive family rehearses add to a feeling of having a place and acknowledgment for each relative.

Setting practical assumptions is an even minded methodology for encouraging acknowledgment inside the nuclear family. Perceiving that every relative has novel qualities, difficulties, and approaches to drawing in with the world mitigates dissatisfaction and frustration. Laying out clear and feasible assumptions adds to a strong climate, permitting every person, incorporating the one with mental imbalance, to flourish in their own specific manner.

Advancing a qualities based point of view is a groundbreaking system in encouraging acknowledgment. Recognizing and commending the one of a kind capacities and gifts of the person with mental imbalance reevaluates the story from a shortfall based model to one that values neurodiversity. Relatives can effectively distinguish and sustain the qualities of their medically introverted family member, encouraging a climate where everybody's commitments are perceived and appreciated.

Empowering self-backing inside the nuclear family engages the person with chemical imbalance to convey their requirements, inclinations, and limits. This procedure includes encouraging autonomy, showing self-promotion abilities, and giving open doors to the person to articulate their thoughts. By developing self-promotion, families add to a feeling of organization and independence for the medically introverted relative, encouraging acknowledgment through common regard.

Carrying out reliable schedules and designs adds to a feeling of consistency and security inside the nuclear family, helping people with chemical imbalance who might track down solace in everyday practice. Laying out clear timetables and schedules establishes a climate where assumptions are straightforward, diminishing nervousness and stress. Consistency inside the relational intricacy adds to a feeling that everything is good and acknowledgment for all interested parties.

Empowering shared encounters and exercises reinforces the bonds inside the nuclear family. Finding normal interests and participating in exercises that take special care of the different inclinations of every relative encourages a feeling of association. These common encounters set out open doors for figuring out, collaboration, and shared pleasure, adding to a comprehensive family culture that advances acknowledgment.

Executing uplifting feedback and commendation is a strong technique for cultivating acknowledgment inside the family. Perceiving and commending accomplishments, both of all shapes and sizes, adds to a positive and steady air. Uplifting feedback spurs the person with mental imbalance as well as supports a culture of consolation and appreciation inside the nuclear family, fortifying the obligations of acknowledgment.

Looking for outer help through treatment, directing, or support bunches is a significant methodology for cultivating acknowledgment inside the family. Proficient direction furnishes families with the instruments to explore difficulties, upgrade correspondence, and foster techniques custom-made to their extraordinary circumstance. Support bunches offer a stage for sharing encounters and experiences, cultivating a feeling of local area that can be instrumental in the excursion toward acknowledgment.

Empowering a funny bone inside the nuclear family can be a happy yet significant procedure for cultivating acknowledgment. Humor can diffuse strain, make snapshots of euphoria, and energize an uplifting perspective. Finding snapshots of levity in the midst of difficulties assists relatives with adapting to pressure and cultivates an environment where acknowledgment is combined with versatility and a capacity to explore the intricacies of residing with chemical imbalance.

Developing a development outlook inside the family adds to a positive and versatile way to deal with difficulties. Embracing that capacities and abilities can be created after some time empowers a family culture that values progress and exertion. A development outlook encourages versatility, flexibility, and a confidence in the potential for development and improvement, adding to a climate where acknowledgment is combined with idealism.

Empowering singularity inside the nuclear family is a procedure that perceives and praises the special characteristics of every relative. Cultivating a climate where contrasts are embraced instead of limited advances acknowledgment. This includes perceiving and regarding individual limits, considering individual articulation, and valuing the variety that every relative brings to the dynamic.

Executing clear and steady limits is a fundamental system for encouraging acknowledgment inside the family. Obviously characterized assumptions and limits add to a feeling of request and security, giving strength to all relatives. Laying out and keeping up with limits guarantees that everybody's requirements are regarded, adding to a climate where acknowledgment is established in an underpinning of shared understanding.

Advancing a culture of persistence inside the nuclear family is a basic methodology for encouraging acknowledgment. Living with chemical imbalance might include exploring one of a kind difficulties and snapshots of trouble. Developing persistence permits relatives to move toward these difficulties with understanding and sympathy, adding to a climate where acknowledgment is combined with a feeling of shared perseverance.

Praising neurodiversity inside the nuclear family is a comprehensive and enveloping system for cultivating acknowledgment. Embracing that neurological contrasts are a characteristic variety of the human experience difficulties cultural standards and advances a comprehensive mentality. Commending neurodiversity includes effectively testing marks of shame, upholding for acknowledgment past the nuclear family, and adding to a more extensive cultural shift towards embracing contrasts.

All in all, encouraging acknowledgment inside the nuclear family when a part has mental imbalance is a dynamic and complex excursion that includes a blend of techniques. From open correspondence and training to establishing comprehensive conditions and advancing independence, these systems add to a climate where each relative is esteemed and acknowledged. The aggregate effect of these procedures is extraordinary, making a family culture established in figuring out, sympathy, and a festival of neurodiversity. As families execute these procedures, they support acknowledgment inside their own elements as well as add to a more extensive cultural development towards inclusivity and understanding for people with chemical imbalance.

Chapter 3

Early Steps: Navigating Childhood

Youth denotes an essential stage in the excursion of families exploring chemical imbalance range jumble (ASD), and the encounters during this period shape the direction of grasping, acknowledgment, and backing. "Early Advances: Exploring Youth" is a story that unfurls with a rich embroidery of difficulties and wins, enlightening the special elements families experience as they leave on the beginning phases of their excursion with a kid on the range.

The initial steps on this excursion frequently start with the acknowledgment of formative contrasts. Guardians might notice unobtrusive signs or notice defers in achievements, provoking worries that lead to looking for proficient direction. The method involved with getting a precise finding turns into a urgent starting step, establishing the groundwork for grasping the interesting requirements and qualities of the kid. Exploring this early territory requires strength and a promise to unwinding the secrets of mental imbalance, as families wrestle with the ramifications of a conclusion that makes way for the excursion ahead.

Early mediations arise as a foundation in the early strides of exploring youth with mental imbalance. The quest for customized helpful methodologies, discourse and language mediations, and formative help becomes vital. Families participate in a bunch of treatments pointed toward tending to explicit difficulties, advancing relational abilities, and encouraging social turn of events.

The victories inside this setting lie in seeing the kid's advancement, praising achievements accomplished through mediations, and developing a feeling of positive thinking about the potential for development and improvement.

The youth venture is set apart by a nuanced dance between the delight of commending accomplishments and the difficulties of exploring formative inconsistencies. Families frequently end up flipping between snapshots of happiness, like a youngster's previously verbally expressed words or effective social collaborations, and the consciousness of novel obstacles related with mental imbalance. This fragile equilibrium requests profound versatility and a capacity to see the value in the little triumphs while recognizing the intricacies of the formative scene.

Relational intricacies go through change during these early strides, as kin, guardians, and more distant family individuals adjust to the real factors of living with chemical imbalance. Kin, specifically, assume a critical part in this developing story. The youth venture includes encouraging comprehension among kin, tending to expected sensations of disarray or contention, and developing bonds that go past the regular kin dynamic. The victories in this setting are reflected in the development of steady kin connections and a common obligation to the prosperity of the youngster on the range.

Besides, youth turns into a phase for molding insights inside the more distant family. Grandparents, aunties, uncles, and cousins add to the familial encouraging group of people, and their comprehension of mental imbalance assumes a crucial part in cultivating acknowledgment. The story unfurls as families effectively take part in training and mindfulness endeavors, dissipating fantasies, and advancing a culture of inclusivity inside the more distant family. Wins arise as relatives rally together, offering backing, understanding, and an aggregate obligation to the youngster's formative process.

Early schooling settings become a critical field in the excursion through youth with mental imbalance. Families explore the intricacies of finding comprehensive instructive conditions that oblige the remarkable learning styles of their youngster. Teaming up with teachers, pushing for individualized learning plans, and encouraging a comprehensive study hall air become focal parts of the early advances. The victories inside this instructive scene are seen in the youngster's scholarly advancement, the improvement of interactive abilities, and the development of a comprehensive mentality inside the instructive local area.

The youth account stretches out past conventional schooling to envelop the more extensive local area. Families end up taking part in support, bringing issues to light, and testing cultural discernments about chemical imbalance. Early advances include effectively taking part in discussions that encourage understanding, disperse generalizations, and add to a more comprehensive local area. Wins in this setting arise as families witness a change in cultural mentalities, preparing for more noteworthy acknowledgment and backing for people with chemical imbalance.

Tactile encounters become a point of convergence in the early strides of young life with mental imbalance. The youngster's elevated or lessened aversions to tactile upgrades present interesting difficulties and valuable open doors for understanding. Families figure out how to explore tactile responsive qualities, adjusting conditions to oblige the kid's necessities, and cultivating a tangible well disposed home. Wins in this domain are reflected in the production of strong conditions that add to the kid's solace, prosperity, and generally speaking formative advancement.

Early advances include facing likely cultural marks of disgrace and misinterpretations related with mental imbalance. Families become advocates, dissipating legends, and effectively captivating in drives that challenge generalizations. The victories inside this backing scene lie in the steady destroying of marks of disgrace, expanded mindfulness, and the production of a more merciful society that embraces neurodiversity. Families become impetuses for more extensive social change, adding to a story that perceives and commends the novel commitments of people with chemical imbalance.

Changing from youth to immaturity turns into a huge section in the story. Families explore the intricacies of pre-adulthood with a consciousness of the exceptional difficulties that people with mental imbalance might look during this stage. The early strides of puberty include tending to social subtleties, encouraging freedom, and supporting the youngster's excursion of self-revelation. Wins in this period are seen in the improvement of interactive abilities, the development of fellowships, and the development of a feeling of character inside the juvenile on the range.

Early adulthood unfurls as families explore the progress from pre-adulthood, confronting new difficulties connected with work, advanced education, and free living. The early strides in adulthood include pushing for comprehensive open doors, addressing obstructions to section into the labor force, and supporting the person in their quest for significant and satisfying grown-up lives. Wins arise as families witness the effective change of their youngster into adulthood, outfitted with the abilities and backing important for free living.

The profound scene inside the early strides of young life with chemical imbalance is many-sided, set apart by a range of feelings going from euphoria and pride to snapshots of disappointment and concern. Families experience the significant effect of the kid's excursion on their own profound prosperity, requesting strength and a versatile attitude. Wins in this profound territory are reflected in the getting through bonds inside the family, the festival of shared triumphs, and the development of a climate where love and acknowledgment rise above the difficulties.

Diversity adds profundity to the youth story, perceiving that encounters are molded by chemical imbalance as well as by variables like orientation, race, and financial status. Families explore the novel difficulties related with interconnection, pushing for inclusivity and tending to abberations inside the chemical imbalance local area. Wins arise as families effectively add to a story that recognizes and regards different voices, cultivating a more impartial and grasping society.

All in all, "Early Advances: Exploring Youth" is a story that unfurls with an intricacy that reflects the formative scene of youngsters with mental imbalance and their families. The early advances include difficulties that request strength, versatility, and support, yet they likewise incorporate victories that celebrate achievements, cultivate understanding, and add to a more extensive cultural shift towards acknowledgment. As families explore the beginning phases of life as a youngster with chemical imbalance, they become dynamic members in a story that rises above individual encounters, molding the scene for people in the future and encouraging a world that embraces neurodiversity.

3.1 Understanding early signs and diagnosis of autism.

Seeing early signs and the ensuing finding of chemical imbalance is a basic excursion that starts with the nuanced perception of a youngster's formative achievements. The story unfurls as families and guardians set out on a cycle that includes perceiving unobtrusive markers, looking for proficient direction, and at last getting a precise determination that lays the preparation for custom fitted help and intercession.

Early indications of chemical imbalance frequently manifest in the formative spaces of correspondence, social collaboration, and conduct. In the domain of correspondence, guardians might see delays or abnormal themes, like restricted prattling, an absence of reaction in their possession, or troubles with expressive language. In the social circle, signs might appear as difficulties in shaping associations with peers, restricted eye to eye connection, or an apathy toward shared exercises. Social pointers can incorporate redundant developments, emphasis on schedules, and aversions to tactile upgrades. Understanding these early signs requires sharp perception and a consciousness of the assorted manners by which chemical imbalance can show.

The excursion toward conclusion normally starts with an elevated mindfulness with respect to guardians or parental figures. It includes perceiving that a kid's formative direction varies from run of the mill designs and may warrant further examination. The choice to look for proficient direction frequently rises up out of a blend of parental instinct, perceptions via guardians, and contribution from pediatricians or instructors. The acknowledgment of early signs turns into a urgent second, making way for the family's proactive commitment to the indicative cycle.

Looking for proficient direction includes teaming up with medical services suppliers and experts who can lead a far reaching evaluation. The demonstrative interaction for chemical imbalance is multidisciplinary, including experts like pediatricians, formative clinicians, discourse and language specialists, and word related advisors. The story unfurls as families explore arrangements, share their perceptions, and take part in appraisals that expect to thoroughly catch the youngster's formative profile. The demonstrative excursion requests persistence, open correspondence, and joint effort among parental figures and experts.

Early indications of chemical imbalance might turn out to be more clear during routine well-kid check-ups, inciting pediatricians to start further assessment. Screening devices and normalized evaluations become instrumental in recognizing formative contrasts and giving a benchmark to the symptomatic cycle. The contribution of trained professionals, like formative clinicians, further refines the evaluation, considering a nuanced comprehension of the youngster's assets, difficulties, and explicit qualities related with mental imbalance.

The excursion toward a chemical imbalance finding is set apart by the acknowledgment of the assorted manners by which mental imbalance can show. The range idea of mental imbalance implies that people might give a large number of capacities, difficulties, and remarkable profiles. The indicative interaction plans to catch this variety, giving families an extensive comprehension of their youngster's particular assets and regions that might profit from designated help. Perceiving the uniqueness of every person on the range turns into a focal subject in the excursion toward determination.

The profound scene during the indicative interaction is intricate, set apart by a range of sentiments going from vulnerability and uneasiness to a liberating sensation and approval. Families wrestle with the possible effect of a mental imbalance conclusion on their youngster's future, and the cycle requests close to home flexibility. The account unfurls as families explore these feelings, looking for help from experts, associating with different families on comparative excursions, and effectively captivating in taking care of oneself to explore the intricacies of the demonstrative territory.

Besides, social contemplations assume a critical part in the comprehension and acknowledgment of a chemical imbalance determination. Social convictions, standards, and perspectives toward neurodiversity impact the manner in which families see and move toward the analytic excursion. The account extends to envelop the multifacetedness of social foundations, underlining the significance of socially able and comprehensive demonstrative practices. Perceiving and regarding different viewpoints inside the symptomatic cycle adds to a story that qualities and praises the lavishness of social variety inside the mental imbalance local area.

The excursion toward a mental imbalance determination isn't static; it advances as families effectively participate in the resulting steps of understanding and exploring the ramifications of the finding. When the determination is gotten, families frequently experience a double story — a feeling of clearness and understanding combined with the acknowledgment of the difficulties that lie ahead. Understanding the finding includes handling the data given by experts, looking for extra assets, and effectively taking part in the definition of an individualized mediation plan.

Early mediation turns into a focal concentration in the story of understanding and answering a chemical imbalance finding. Families take part in a cooperative cycle with advisors, teachers, and mediation experts to plan and execute designated techniques that address the kid's novel requirements. Early mediation incorporates a scope of remedial methodologies, including discourse and language treatment, word related treatment, applied conduct examination (ABA), and interactive abilities intercessions. The story of early intercession is set apart by a pledge to cultivating the kid's turn of events and boosting their true capacity during this significant stage.

Understanding the ramifications of a chemical imbalance conclusion includes wrestling with the cultural insights and marks of disgrace related with neurodevelopmental contrasts. Families become advocates, testing generalizations, and effectively partaking in mindfulness drives that add to a more comprehensive and compassionate society. The story reaches out past the nuclear family to envelop more extensive local area commitment, cultivating understanding and acknowledgment inside instructive foundations, medical services settings, and cultural spaces.

The excursion of seeing early signs and getting a mental imbalance conclusion is interlaced with the continuous obligation to support and mindfulness. Families frequently end up at the front of dissipating legends, advancing neurodiversity, and pushing for comprehensive practices. The story grows to envelop the more extensive cultural scene, underscoring the job of families as problem solvers in testing marks of shame and encouraging a culture that praises the exceptional qualities and commitments of people with chemical imbalance.

Instructive settings become huge fields for understanding and answering a mental imbalance finding. Families explore the intricacies of finding comprehensive instructive conditions that perceive and oblige the assorted learning styles of their kid. Working together with instructors, upholding for individualized schooling plans (IEPs), and encouraging a comprehensive study hall air become vital parts of the account. The victories inside this instructive scene are seen in the kid's scholastic advancement, the improvement of interactive abilities, and the development of a comprehensive attitude inside the instructive local area.

Encouraging groups of people and networks assume a vital part in the continuous story of understanding and answering a chemical imbalance finding. Families interface with different guardians, parental figures, and people on the range, making a strong biological system that cultivates shared encounters and bits of knowledge.

The story grows to incorporate the voices of people with mental imbalance, who become dynamic members in forming the talk encompassing neurodiversity. Understanding the determination includes embracing different points of view and adding to an aggregate story that esteems the extravagance of the mental imbalance local area.

Progressing through various phases of life as a youngster, youthfulness, and adulthood turns out to be important for the continuous story of understanding and answering a chemical imbalance conclusion. Families adjust to the developing requirements of their kid, exploring the intricacies of social cooperations, freedom, and the quest for individual personality during pre-adulthood. The story stretches out to incorporate the difficulties and wins of adulthood, including open doors for business, advanced education, and free living. Understanding the determination turns into a continuous interaction that includes adjusting methodologies and mediations to line up with the changing requirements and goals of the person on the range.

All in all, the story of seeing early signs and getting a chemical imbalance finding is a dynamic and complex excursion that reaches out past the underlying acknowledgment of formative contrasts. It includes exploring a complicated landscape set apart by profound subtleties, social contemplations, and progressing obligation to promotion and mindfulness.

The account unfurls as families effectively take part during the time spent grasping, looking for help, and molding a comprehensive and sympathetic culture that praises the variety of neurodevelopmental encounters. As families add to this continuous story, they become instrumental in encouraging a world that perceives and esteems the exceptional qualities and commitments of people with chemical imbalance.

3.2 Parenting strategies for nurturing a child on the spectrum.

Nurturing a kid on the chemical imbalance range is a one of a kind excursion that requires a nuanced and versatile methodology. Sustaining a youngster with chemical imbalance includes embracing their distinction, figuring out their particular requirements, and cultivating a climate that upholds their development and improvement. The story of nurturing techniques for a youngster on the range unfurls with a mix of persistence, backing, and a guarantee to making a steady and comprehensive relational peculiarity.

Persistence turns into a foundation of nurturing methodologies for a youngster on the range. Youngsters with chemical imbalance might have exceptional correspondence styles, tangible responsive qualities, and personal conduct standards that request a patient and figuring out approach. Guardians explore the complexities of these distinctions, perceiving that progress might unfurl at its own speed. Persistence isn't simply an ideals; a useful instrument permits guardians to establish a climate where the kid feels upheld, acknowledged, and urged to investigate their true capacity.

Understanding and embracing the independence of a youngster on the mental imbalance range is vital to powerful nurturing. Every kid has their own assets, difficulties, and inclinations. Guardians effectively take part in noticing and grasping their kid's special profile, perceiving the variety inside the range. This understanding structures the reason for custom fitted nurturing techniques that take care of the particular necessities and interests of the youngster, making a customized approach that lines up with their formative process.

Compelling correspondence turns into a fundamental part of nurturing procedures for a youngster on the range. Youngsters with mental imbalance might have difficulties in expressive and responsive correspondence, expecting guardians to investigate elective methods of connection. Visual backings, social stories, and augmentative correspondence frameworks become important apparatuses in working with correspondence. Guardians become capable at perceiving and answering their youngster's correspondence signals, establishing an acformative climate that overcomes any issues between different correspondence styles.

Establishing a tactile cordial climate is a commonsense and effective nurturing technique for a youngster on the range. Tactile responsive qualities are normal among people with mental imbalance, and guardians effectively take part in distinguishing and tending to tangible triggers. This includes adjusting the home climate to limit tangible over-burden, giving tactile breaks, and integrating tactile cordial components into day to day schedules. The production of a tactile cordial space cultivates a feeling of solace and security for the youngster, adding to their general prosperity.

Organized schedules and visual timetables become fundamental parts of nurturing methodologies for a youngster with mental imbalance. Consistency and routine deal a feeling of safety and solidness for youngsters on the range, assisting them explore day to day exercises no sweat. Guardians cooperatively make and keep up with schedules, utilizing visual timetables to give clear assumptions and changes. This organized methodology adds to a more coordinated and amicable relational peculiarity, decreasing pressure and nervousness for the two guardians and the kid.

Promotion is a critical component of nurturing procedures for a kid on the range. Guardians effectively take part in upholding for their youngster's necessities inside different settings, including instructive organizations, medical care, and local area spaces. This includes teaming up with instructors, medical services experts, and local area individuals to guarantee that the kid gets the vital help and facilities. Promotion reaches out past individual communications to add to a more extensive cultural shift toward understanding and inclusivity.

Interactive abilities improvement turns into a point of convergence in nurturing procedures for a youngster on the range. Youngsters with mental imbalance might confront difficulties in understanding and exploring social communications, and guardians assume a crucial part in cultivating interactive abilities improvement.

This includes setting out open doors for socialization, showing express meaningful gestures, and giving direction on exploring social subtleties. Guardians effectively take part in working with fellowships, advancing companion associations, and sustaining the kid's social associations inside the family and local area.

Uplifting feedback and support are incredible assets in nurturing a kid with chemical imbalance. Recognizing and commending accomplishments, regardless of how little, add to a positive and strong family air. Guardians effectively participate in distinguishing and supporting the youngster's assets, cultivating an identity viability and certainty. Uplifting feedback stretches out past customary award frameworks to incorporate verbal acclaim, affirmation of exertion, and the festival of the youngster's extraordinary achievements.

Building serious areas of strength for an organization turns into a fundamental part of nurturing procedures for a youngster on the range. Guardians effectively look for associations with different families, support gatherings, and experts who represent considerable authority in chemical imbalance. The encouraging group of people gives a stage to sharing encounters, experiences, and assets. Guardians become advocates for their own youngster as well as for the more extensive mental imbalance local area, adding to an aggregate story that values neurodiversity and cultivates understanding.

Instructive promotion is a critical part of nurturing procedures for a kid with chemical imbalance. Guardians team up with instructors to establish a comprehensive and strong instructive climate that takes care of the kid's exceptional learning style. This includes effectively taking part in Individualized Training System (IEP) gatherings, upholding for essential facilities, and cultivating an organization with educators and school staff. Instructive promotion stretches out past the proper study hall to envelop a comprehensive methodology that perceives and upholds the youngster's different capacities and qualities.

Advancing freedom is a progressive and fundamental part of nurturing techniques for a youngster on the range. Guardians effectively participate in showing fundamental abilities, cultivating self improvement capacities, and empowering the kid to take on age-proper obligations. The excursion toward freedom includes perceiving and praising the kid's developing independence, fabricating an establishment for their future progress in different parts of day to day existence. Guardians offset help and support with open doors for the kid to investigate and foster their freedom.

Developing a development outlook inside the family turns into a groundbreaking nurturing technique. Embracing the conviction that capacities and abilities can be created over the long haul encourages a culture of positive thinking, versatility, and flexibility. Guardians effectively advance a development mentality by stressing exertion, progress, and the growing experience. This approach adds to a relational peculiarity where difficulties are seen as any open doors for development, establishing a climate that sustains the youngster's true capacity and cultivates a feeling of persistent turn of events.

Parental taking care of oneself arises as a fundamental and frequently ignored part of nurturing techniques for a kid on the range. Sustaining a kid with mental imbalance can be genuinely and truly requesting, and guardians effectively focus on their own prosperity. This includes perceiving the significance of taking care of oneself works on, looking for help when required, and making a harmony between providing care liabilities and individual satisfaction. Parental taking care of oneself isn't simply a singular undertaking; it adds to a relational peculiarity where the prosperity of every relative is focused on.

Understanding and overseeing testing ways of behaving is a continuous part of nurturing a youngster on the range. Kids with mental imbalance might display ways of behaving that act as correspondence signals or result from tangible responsive qualities. Guardians effectively take part in recognizing triggers, executing preventive methodologies, and showing the youngster elective strategies for dealing with hardship or stress. The story of overseeing testing ways of behaving includes a mix of persistence, proactive intercession, and a guarantee to grasping the basic reasons for the way of behaving.

Making a kin emotionally supportive network turns into a special and significant nurturing procedure for families with a kid on the range. Kin might explore their own arrangement of difficulties and wins, and guardians effectively cultivate a steady kin dynamic. This includes advancing compassion, working with open correspondence, and giving chances to shared encounters. Kin support stretches out past the close family to incorporate the more extensive local area, adding to a story that esteems the viewpoints and commitments of kin inside the mental imbalance local area.

Innovation and assistive gadgets become important devices in nurturing methodologies for a youngster with chemical imbalance. Guardians investigate the utilization of innovation, including correspondence applications, visual backings, and instructive games, to improve the youngster's learning and correspondence encounters. Assistive gadgets, for example, correspondence sheets or tangible instruments, are incorporated into everyday schedules to offer extra help. The story of innovation use in nurturing mirrors a powerful methodology that embraces creative answers for take special care of the exceptional requirements of the kid.

The story of nurturing techniques for a kid on the range is a developing and dynamic excursion that incorporates a range of encounters, difficulties, and wins. Guardians effectively take part in a cycle that includes understanding and embracing the distinction of their youngster, pushing for their necessities, and establishing a steady family climate. The story reaches out past the nuclear family to add to a more extensive cultural shift toward inclusivity, understanding, and festivity of neurodiversity.

3.3 The importance of early intervention and inclusive education.

The significance of early mediation and comprehensive schooling with regards to kids with assorted needs, including chemical imbalance, is significant and sweeping. These two points of support stand as foundations in encouraging the ideal turn of events, development, and cultural combination of people who might encounter exceptional difficulties. This account investigates the meaning of early mediation and comprehensive schooling, uncovering their groundbreaking effect on the existences of kids and the more extensive local area.

Early mediation becomes the dominant focal point in the account, perceiving the basic window of formative versatility in youth. For youngsters with assorted needs, remembering those for the mental imbalance range, convenient and designated mediations can make ready for significant advancement. Early intercession incorporates a scope of helpful methodologies, including discourse and language treatment, word related treatment, conduct mediations, and interactive abilities preparing. It isn't only a response to challenges yet a proactive and preventive system that expects to address possible formative deferrals, upgrade versatile abilities, and give families the vital instruments and backing.

The story of early intercession unfurls inside a structure that values individual contrasts and perceives the different necessities of kids. Custom-made mediations are intended to line up with the remarkable qualities, difficulties, and inclinations of every kid, encouraging a customized approach that regards neurodiversity. Early intercession goes past tending to explicit shortages; it embraces an all encompassing viewpoint that thinks about the youngster's general prosperity, profound wellbeing, and social turn of events. By interceding early, the story shifts from a shortage based model to one that stresses prospects, potential, and the festival of each and every youngster's remarkable excursion.

The effect of early mediation stretches out past the singular youngster to incorporate their family and local area. Families effectively participate in the mediation cycle, becoming accomplices in their kid's formative process. Early intercession furnishes families with the fundamental abilities, assets, and support to explore the difficulties related with bringing up a youngster with different necessities. The story unfurls as families experience a feeling of strengthening, gain a more profound comprehension of their kid, and effectively add to establishing a climate that sustains the kid's development.

Comprehensive schooling arises as an equal story that supplements and expands the standards of early mediation. Comprehensive training is established in the conviction that all kids, no matter what their capacities or handicaps, reserve the privilege to learn together in standard instructive settings. This story challenges customary thoughts of isolating youngsters in view of their disparities and effectively advocates for an instructive scene that values variety and advances equivalent open doors for all.

The story of comprehensive training destroys hindrances to learning and interest, cultivating a climate where each kid is perceived, esteemed, and furnished with the vital backings. For kids with different requirements, incorporating those with mental imbalance, comprehensive instruction turns into an impetus for social consideration, peer connections, and the improvement of fundamental abilities. The story unfurls as kids on the chemical imbalance range effectively take part in standard homerooms, take part in scholar and social exercises, and foster a feeling of having a place inside the more extensive instructive local area.

Educators assume a crucial part in the story of comprehensive training, becoming supporters for variety and problem solvers inside the homeroom. Comprehensive training provokes instructors to embrace adaptable showing procedures, make open learning materials, and cultivate a comprehensive homeroom culture. Educators effectively take part in proficient advancement to improve how they might interpret different learning styles and obtain the vital apparatuses to help kids with mental imbalance and other assorted needs. The story shifts from an emphasis on deficiencies to an accentuation on establishing conditions that celebrate contrasts, advance acknowledgment, and expand the capability of each and every student.

The story of comprehensive schooling stretches out to the more extensive local area, testing cultural standards and encouraging a culture that values variety. Comprehensive schools become microcosms of a comprehensive society, molding mentalities, discernments, and assumptions. The story unfurls as networks observer the positive effect of comprehensive training, on the youngsters straightforwardly involved as well as on the more extensive social shift toward acknowledgment and understanding. Comprehensive training turns into an incredible asset for separating cultural boundaries and adding to an additional humane and sympathetic world.

The convergence of early mediation and comprehensive instruction makes a cooperative energy that enhances their effect on the existences of youngsters with different necessities. The early recognizable proof and mediation worked with by comprehensive instructive settings make a consistent continuum of help. The account unfurls as youngsters get early help inside the comprehensive homeroom climate, where teachers team up with experts to address explicit necessities. This cooperative methodology guarantees that the kid's extraordinary profile is perceived and obliged, making a firm and incorporated emotionally supportive network that traverses both home and school.

Besides, the story of early mediation and comprehensive training effectively difficulties fundamental imbalances inside the instructive scene. It advocates for approaches and practices that focus on value, access, and inclusivity. The story reaches out past the singular kid to resolve fundamental issues connected with instructor preparing, asset distribution, and the general design of schooling systems. Support turns into a main impetus, molding a story that calls for extraordinary changes inside instructive establishments to establish conditions where each kid can flourish.

The cultural account of early mediation and comprehensive training turns into an account of potential, probability, and progress. It challenges assumptions about what people with different requirements can accomplish and adds to a story that esteems their special commitments. The account unfurls as kids who got early mediations and experienced comprehensive training become dynamic members in the public arena, seeking after advanced education, entering the labor force, and adding to their networks.

The monetary story of early mediation and comprehensive training highlights their drawn out cultural advantages. Putting resources into early mediation programs and comprehensive training yields returns as far as worked on instructive results, decreased reliance on help benefits, and expanded open doors for people with different necessities to contribute definitively to society. The story shifts from review these intercessions as costs to remembering them as speculations with expansive social and monetary profits.

The story of early intercession and comprehensive training turns into a source of inspiration, welcoming partners at different levels to add to the making of a more comprehensive and fair society effectively. Policymakers are asked to authorize regulation that upholds comprehensive practices, assigns assets decisively, and guarantees that the standards of early mediation and comprehensive schooling are implanted in the instructive system. The story calls for progressing proficient improvement for instructors, encouraging a culture of nonstop learning and transformation to the developing necessities of different students.

The account of early mediation and comprehensive instruction effectively includes guardians as backers, accomplices, and drivers of progress inside the school system. Parental voices add to the account by molding approaches, partaking in school advisory groups, and effectively teaming up with teachers to establish comprehensive instructive conditions. Guardians become instrumental in guaranteeing that the standards of early mediation and comprehensive schooling are hypothetical ideas as well as down to earth real factors that shape the regular encounters of their kids.

All in all, the story of early mediation and comprehensive training is a multilayered and dynamic excursion that reaches out past the singular youngster to envelop families, teachers, networks, and society at large. A story challenges obsolete ideal models, advocates for value and inclusivity, and effectively adds to molding a reality where each kid, no matter what their capacities or handicaps, is perceived, esteemed, and furnished with the vital backings to flourish. As this account keeps on developing, it turns into an account of trust, progress, and the extraordinary force of early mediation and comprehensive schooling in making a more sympathetic and comprehensive society.

Chapter 4

Navigating the School Landscape

Exploring the school scene, especially for understudies with different necessities like chemical imbalance, is a complicated excursion that includes a heap of difficulties and wins. This account investigates the multi-layered parts of exploring the school scene for youngsters with chemical imbalance, revealing insight into the encounters of understudies, guardians, instructors, and the more extensive instructive local area.

The excursion starts with the change into the school system, denoting a huge achievement for kids with mental imbalance and their families. The account unfurls as guardians explore the underlying advances, looking for comprehensive and strong instructive conditions for their youngsters. This frequently includes teaming up with instructors, school heads, and experts to guarantee that the school setting is prepared to oblige the novel learning styles and needs of understudies on the chemical imbalance range.

For understudies with mental imbalance, the school scene is a social and tangible minefield that requests strength and versatility. The story investigates the difficulties these understudies face in exploring social associations, tactile improvements, and the scholarly requests of the homeroom. Teachers assume a urgent part in establishing a steady climate that recognizes and addresses these difficulties. This includes executing tangible agreeable works on, giving clear correspondence, and cultivating comprehensive social elements inside the study hall.

Individualized Instruction Projects (IEPs) become a focal part of the story, molding the instructive experience for understudies with mental imbalance. The cooperative course of fostering an IEP includes guardians, instructors, and experts cooperating to fit the instructive way to deal with the exceptional requirements of the understudy. The account unfurls as IEPs become dynamic and advancing records, mirroring the continuous advancement, difficulties, and goals of the understudy all through their instructive excursion.

Educators, as key figures in the school scene, leave on an excursion of understanding and adjusting their helping methodologies to oblige different students, incorporating those with mental imbalance. The story investigates the job of expert turn of events, continuous preparation, and the development of a mentality that embraces inclusivity. Educators effectively take part in making homerooms that celebrate neurodiversity, execute separated guidance, and give the important backings to understudies with different requirements to flourish scholastically and socially.

Peer connections inside the school scene become a huge part of the story. Understudies with chemical imbalance might confront difficulties in shaping and keeping up with fellowships, and the account unfurls as teachers and guardians team up to cultivate comprehensive friend cooperations. Interactive abilities preparing, peer training programs, and a culture of acknowledgment add to a school climate where all understudies, no matter what their neurodiversity, can participate in significant and strong connections.

The story extends to envelop the more extensive school local area, including heads, support staff, and different understudies. School chairmen assume a vital part in forming strategies, distributing assets, and making a culture that focuses on consideration. The story unfurls as heads effectively work to destroy foundational hindrances, advance mindfulness, and cultivate a feeling of having a place for understudies with chemical imbalance inside the school local area. Support staff, including custom curriculum assistants and specialists, become vital accomplices in the instructive excursion, giving designated mediations and backing that supplement the by and large instructive experience.

Comprehensive extracurricular exercises arise as a story string that adds to the all encompassing improvement of understudies with mental imbalance inside the school scene. The account unfurls as schools effectively work to guarantee that extracurricular contributions are comprehensive and open. This might include adjusting exercises, offering extra help, and cultivating a culture that supports the interest of understudies with different requirements. The support in extracurricular exercises turns into a wellspring of pride, expertise improvement, and social commitment for understudies with mental imbalance.

Progressing between instructive levels turns into an essential part in the story of exploring the school scene. The shift from rudimentary to center school, and later to secondary school, includes a unique interaction that requires cautious preparation and joint effort.

The story unfurls as teachers, guardians, and understudies cooperate to explore these changes, guaranteeing coherence in help, tending to new difficulties, and cultivating a feeling of readiness for the developing scholar and social scene.

The story of exploring the school scene effectively includes guardians as backers and accomplices in their youngster's instructive excursion. Guardians team up with instructors to share experiences, give data about their kid's assets and difficulties, and effectively add to the dynamic cycles connected with their kid's schooling. The account unfurls as guardians take part in continuous correspondence with educators, go to class gatherings, and effectively take part in drives that advance inclusivity and figuring out inside the school local area.

The account stretches out past the singular school to incorporate the more extensive school system and strategy scene. Backing turns into a main impetus as guardians, instructors, and partners cooperate to shape strategies that advance comprehensive training, distribute assets decisively, and make foundational changes that benefit understudies with different necessities. The story unfurls as people inside the school system effectively add to a social shift that values neurodiversity, focuses on inclusivity, and perceives the capability of each and every understudy.

Emergency minutes inside the school scene, like occurrences of harassing or absence of figuring out, become vital parts in the story. The story unfurls as instructors and executives address these difficulties head-on, carrying out enemy of tormenting drives, giving responsiveness preparing, and encouraging a culture of compassion and regard inside the school local area. Emergency minutes become open doors for development, training, and the support of a guarantee to establishing a comprehensive and strong instructive climate for all.

The story of exploring the school scene stretches out to post-optional training and professional open doors for understudies with mental imbalance. The change from secondary school to school or professional preparation includes an interesting arrangement of difficulties and contemplations. The story unfurls as teachers and guardians team up to give the essential backings, facilities, and assets to guarantee an effective change and incorporation into post-optional instructive and professional settings.

Past scholastics, the account investigates the advancement of fundamental abilities inside the school scene. Understudies with mental imbalance effectively take part in programs that encourage autonomy, self-support, and the obtaining of functional abilities fundamental for everyday living. The story unfurls as instructors and guardians cooperate to make a far reaching instructive experience that goes past conventional scholastics, planning understudies for the intricacies of grown-up life.

The overall account of exploring the school scene is one of flexibility, coordinated effort, and progress. It is an account of people meeting up — understudies, guardians, instructors, executives, and the more extensive local area — to establish an instructive climate that celebrates variety, perceives potential, and effectively advances inclusivity. The excursion is set apart by difficulties, yet it is likewise described by wins, development, and the aggregate obligation to molding a school scene that qualities and elevates each understudy, no matter what their neurodiversity. As this story keeps on unfurling, it turns into an encouraging sign and a demonstration of the groundbreaking force of inclusivity inside the schooling system.

4.1 Challenges within the educational system for autistic individuals.

The difficulties inside the schooling system for medically introverted people include an intricate scene that includes different partners, foundational factors, and nuanced encounters. This story digs into the diverse components of these difficulties, revealing insight into the obstacles looked by mentally unbalanced understudies, their families, teachers, and the more extensive instructive local area.

The excursion starts with the recognizable proof and comprehension of chemical imbalance inside the school system. The story unfurls as teachers and executives wrestle with fluctuating degrees of mindfulness and information about chemical imbalance range jumble (ASD). Restricted preparing and proficient improvement open doors in numerous instructive settings add to an absence of understanding about the different manners by which chemical imbalance can show. This information hole turns into a primary test that shapes the in general instructive experience for mentally unbalanced understudies.

The test of misperceptions and generalizations inside the school system turns into a huge string in the story. Mentally unbalanced people frequently face cultural generalizations that might impact the impression of instructors, friends, and even guardians. These generalizations can propagate misguided judgments about the capacities, potential, and social capacities of mentally unbalanced understudies. The story unfurls as instructors and heads effectively work to challenge these generalizations, advance precise data, and make a comprehensive culture that embraces the remarkable qualities of mentally unbalanced people.

The story extends to incorporate the difficulties connected with early ID and intercession inside the school system. Early indications of mental imbalance may not be promptly perceived, prompting postponed intercession and backing. The story unfurls as families explore a symptomatic excursion that might be full of deferrals, vulnerability, and an absence of assets. The effect of deferred recognizable proof on early mediation turns into a focal test, as opportune help is vital in molding the formative direction of mentally unbalanced understudies.

When recognized, medically introverted understudies frequently experience difficulties connected with the turn of events and execution of Individualized Instruction Projects (IEPs). The account investigates the intricacies of making IEPs that genuinely meet the remarkable requirements of every understudy. Restricted assets, deficient care staff, and an absence of particular preparation add to the difficulties looked by teachers in fitting IEPs to address the particular qualities and difficulties of mentally unbalanced understudies. The story unfurls as guardians become advocates, exploring the regulatory intricacies to guarantee that their kid's IEP is extensive, viable, and helpful for their instructive achievement.

In the scholastic domain, challenges connected with tactile responsive qualities and learning styles become unmistakable elements of the account. Mentally unbalanced understudies might encounter hardships in adjusting to the tactile upgrades present in regular instructive settings. The story unfurls as teachers work to make tactile cordial homerooms, carry out individualized facilities, and cultivate a comprehension of the different manners by which medically introverted under-studies process data. The test reaches out past the study hall to state administered testing, where the unbending design and tangible requests might present huge obstacles for mentally unbalanced people.

Social difficulties inside the school system become a focal story string. Mentally unbalanced understudies frequently face challenges in exploring social connections, framing kinships, and figuring out friendly subtleties. The story unfurls as teachers effectively participate in establishing comprehensive social conditions, executing interactive abilities preparing projects, and cultivating peer training drives. The test reaches out to tending to harassing and advancing a culture of acknowledgment and sympathy inside the school local area.

Correspondence challenges arise as an unavoidable part of the story. Mentally unbalanced understudies might encounter hardships in expressive and open corre-spondence, blocking their capacity to partake in homeroom exercises completely. The account unfurls as teachers investigate elective specialized techniques, carry out augmentative and elective correspondence (AAC) procedures, and establish conditions that work with compelling correspondence for mentally unbalanced understudies. The test reaches out to advancing a more extensive comprehension of different correspondence styles inside the instructive local area.

Changes inside the schooling system become huge difficulties for medically in-troverted understudies. The story unfurls as understudies progress between grade levels, from rudimentary to center school, and from secondary school to post-optional instruction or professional settings. These advances include changes in schedules, assumptions, and social elements, presenting novel difficulties for men-tally unbalanced people who flourish with consistency and schedule. The account stretches out to the more extensive local area, where mindfulness and backing for effective advances become basic parts of making a comprehensive instructive scene.

The story of difficulties inside the school system converges with issues of inclusiv-ity and variety. The absence of portrayal and consideration of mentally unbalanced voices inside the educational plan turns into a striking test. The account unfurls as teachers effectively work to integrate different points of view, encounters, and commitments of medically introverted people into the instructive substance. The test stretches out to making a comprehensive educational plan that goes past tokenistic portrayals and cultivates a veritable appreciation for neurodiversity.

The deficiency of prepared and concentrated work force inside the schooling system arises as an unavoidable test. The account investigates the effect of deficient care staff, including custom curriculum educators, language teachers, and word related advisors, on the general nature of training for medically introverted under-studies. The lack adds to expanded responsibilities, restricted accessibility of indi-vidualized help, and difficulties in gathering the different requirements of mentally unbalanced people inside the homeroom setting.

Inclusivity inside extracurricular exercises turns into an extra story string in the difficulties looked by mentally unbalanced understudies. Restricted openness, an absence of mindfulness, and social boundaries might block the support of mentally unbalanced people in sports, expressions, and other extracurricular pursuits. The story unfurls as schools effectively work to make comprehensive extracurricular projects, give fundamental facilities, and cultivate a culture that energizes the investment, everything being equal, regardless of their neurodiversity.

The story stretches out to the difficulties looked by guardians as supporters inside the schooling system. Guardians frequently end up exploring regulatory obstacles, pushing for proper facilities, and tending to misinterpretations about chemical imbalance. The account unfurls as guardians become vital accomplices in molding comprehensive instructive conditions, effectively partaking in school gatherings, and upholding for fundamental changes that benefit their kid as well as the more extensive mentally unbalanced local area.

The absence of normalized and predictable practices across instructive establishments adds to the difficulties looked by medically introverted people. The story investigates the fluctuation in approaches, facilities, and assets accessible in various schools and regions. This absence of consistency impedes the improvement of best practices, makes variations in instructive encounters, and postures difficulties for understudies who might progress between various instructive settings.

Social contemplations inside the school system become a significant part of the account. The difficulties looked by medically introverted people are affected by social convictions, standards, and perspectives toward neurodiversity. The story unfurls as teachers effectively participate in socially skilled works on, perceiving and regarding different viewpoints inside the instructive local area. The test stretches out to making a comprehensive instructive culture that qualities and praises the lavishness of social variety inside the mental imbalance local area.

The story of difficulties inside the school system turns into a source of inspiration for fundamental change. Backing arises as a main thrust, with guardians, instructors, and partners cooperating to shape strategies, distribute assets decisively, and make an instructive scene that focuses on inclusivity and understanding. The story unfurls as people inside the school system effectively add to a social shift that values neurodiversity, challenges generalizations, and perceives the capability of each and every understudy.

All in all, the story of difficulties inside the schooling system for mentally unbalanced people is a mind boggling and dynamic excursion that includes a large number of elements. It is an account of fundamental holes, misinterpretations, and obstacles that influence the instructive encounters of mentally unbalanced understudies, their families, and the more extensive instructive local area. As this story keeps on unfurling, it turns into an aggregate call to address these difficulties, cultivate inclusivity, and make an instructive scene that qualities and inspires each understudy, no matter what their neurodiversity.

4.2 Successful models of inclusive education.

Effective models of comprehensive schooling exemplify an extraordinary methodology that goes past customary standards to establish conditions where each understudy, no matter what their capacities or handicaps, is esteemed, upheld, and gave equivalent open doors. This story investigates the attributes, standards, and effect of fruitful models of comprehensive training, revealing insight into their extraordinary power inside the instructive scene.

At the core of fruitful models of comprehensive instruction lies a pledge to the major standard of inclusivity. These models challenge the idea of isolating understudies in light of their capacities and embrace the conviction that variety is a strength that improves the instructive experience for everybody. The story unfurls as teachers, executives, and partners effectively work to destroy hindrances, cultivate understanding, and make a culture that perceives and celebrates neurodiversity inside the school local area.

One of the vital mainstays of effective models of comprehensive schooling is the arrangement of fitting help systems. This help goes past simple convenience; it includes grasping the exceptional necessities of every understudy and executing designated mediations that work with their dynamic cooperation in the growing experience. The story investigates the significance of customized help plans, individualized schooling programs (IEPs), and the coordinated effort among general and specialized curriculum educators to establish a comprehensive learning climate that tends to the different requirements, everything being equal.

Cooperation turns into a focal story string in fruitful models of comprehensive training. This includes a powerful organization between broad schooling educators, custom curriculum instructors, support staff, and experts to make a comprehensive instructive biological system on the whole. The account unfurls as instructors team up to share skill, execute separated guidance, and altogether issue address to meet the different advancing necessities of understudies. Cooperative arranging becomes a training as well as a social standard that shapes the comprehensive ethos of the whole school local area.

Proficient improvement arises as a foundation in the story of effective models of comprehensive schooling. Instructors effectively participate in continuous preparation that upgrades how they might interpret different learning styles, outfits them with compelling showing procedures, and encourages a mentality that values inclusivity. The story unfurls as expert improvement turns into a constant excursion, adjusting to developing instructive practices, research discoveries, and the changing necessities of understudies inside a comprehensive structure.

A basic part of fruitful models of comprehensive instruction is the production of tangible cordial conditions. These conditions perceive and address the tactile responsive qualities of understudies, incorporating those with mental imbalance. The story investigates how instructors adjust homeroom settings, execute tangible breaks, and give tactile devices to make comprehensive spaces where all understudies can flourish. The accentuation on tactile well disposed rehearses mirrors a guarantee to obliging different requirements and encouraging an all encompassing way to deal with inclusivity.

Versatile and adaptable educational plan configuration turns into a story string that shapes fruitful models of comprehensive instruction. Teachers effectively work to make educational plans that are receptive to the different learning styles and capacities of understudies. The story unfurls as instructors adjust educational materials, integrate different viewpoints, and carry out innovation to make an educational program that obliges as well as celebrates neurodiversity. This approach difficulties conventional ideas of normalized schooling and embraces a more understudy focused and comprehensive opportunity for growth.

Peer backing and mentorship become indispensable parts of effective models of comprehensive schooling. The story investigates how understudies effectively partake in cultivating a culture of acknowledgment, sympathy, and backing inside the school local area. Peer mentorship programs, mate frameworks, and comprehensive extracurricular exercises add to establishing a climate where understudies with assorted needs are incorporated as well as effectively embraced by their friends. The story unfurls as these connections stretch out past the study hall, forming a school culture that values inclusivity as a common obligation.

Parental contribution arises as a story topic inside fruitful models of comprehensive training. Guardians become dynamic accomplices in the instructive excursion of their youngsters, working together with teachers, going to IEP gatherings, and effectively partaking in drives that advance inclusivity. The story unfurls as guardians contribute their bits of knowledge, advocate for the necessities of their youngsters, and effectively take part in molding the comprehensive culture of the school local area. This joint effort reaches out past individual connections to add to a more extensive social shift inside the instructive scene.

Models of comprehensive training effectively challenge the fundamental boundaries and strategies that upset inclusivity inside the school system. The account investigates how fruitful models advocate for strategy changes, asset assignment, and the improvement of comprehensive practices at the fundamental level. Promotion turns into a main impetus, molding a story that calls for groundbreaking changes inside instructive foundations to establish conditions where each understudy can flourish.

The effect of fruitful models of comprehensive training stretches out past the quick school local area to add to a more extensive cultural shift. The story unfurls as alumni of comprehensive training programs become dynamic members in the public eye, testing cultural standards, and adding to a culture that values variety and inclusivity. The examples of overcoming adversity of people who experienced comprehensive training become strong stories that supporter for the extension of comprehensive practices inside the more extensive instructive scene.

The monetary account inside effective models of comprehensive training accentuates the drawn out cultural advantages. Putting resources into comprehensive schooling isn't simply a moral goal; a monetary speculation yields returns as far as worked on instructive results, diminished reliance on help benefits, and expanded open doors for people with different requirements to contribute genuinely to society. The story shifts from survey inclusivity as an expense to remembering it as a speculation with sweeping social and financial profits.

Social ability turns into a fundamental story subject inside effective models of comprehensive training. The story unfurls as instructors effectively work to make an educational program that mirrors the variety of the understudy body, consolidates socially responsive showing practices, and encourages an environment of regard for all foundations. Comprehensive training models effectively challenge predispositions, generalizations, and foundational imbalances, adding to a more extensive social shift toward understanding and embracing variety.

Innovation joining turns into a powerful story string inside fruitful models of comprehensive training. The story investigates how innovation is utilized to establish comprehensive learning conditions, give elective method for correspondence, and proposition customized opportunities for growth. Assistive innovations become significant devices that upgrade availability and oblige assorted learning styles. The story unfurls as innovation is incorporated into the educational program to make a more comprehensive and versatile instructive experience.

Effective models of comprehensive training effectively take part in continuous appraisal and reflection. The story investigates how instructors and overseers evaluate the viability of comprehensive practices, assemble criticism from understudies and guardians, and ponder approaches to further develop inclusivity inside the school system constantly. The obligation to progressing appraisal and reflection guarantees that effective models stay dynamic, responsive, and versatile to the advancing requirements of understudies and the more extensive instructive local area.

All in all, the story of fruitful models of comprehensive schooling is an account of extraordinary change, cooperation, and a guarantee to establishing instructive conditions that commend variety and encourage inclusivity. A story challenges customary ideal models, advocates for foundational changes, and effectively adds to a social shift inside the instructive scene. As this story keeps on unfurling, it turns into an encouraging sign and a demonstration of the extraordinary force of comprehensive schooling in forming a more evenhanded, sympathetic, and comprehensive society.

4.3 Empowering educators to support neurodiverse students.

Engaging instructors to help neurodiverse understudies is a multi-layered venture that includes cultivating a culture of understanding, giving designated preparing, and establishing comprehensive conditions inside instructive organizations. This story investigates the basic job of teachers in supporting neurodiverse understudies, the difficulties they might experience, and the engaging procedures that add to a more comprehensive instructive scene.

At the center of engaging teachers is the acknowledgment and festivity of neurodiversity. This story unfurls as teachers embrace the comprehension that neurodiverse understudies, incorporating those with chemical imbalance, ADHD, dyslexia, and other neurodevelopmental contrasts, bring extraordinary viewpoints, qualities, and gifts to the homeroom. The shift from a deficiency based model to a resource based point of view turns into a fundamental guideline, molding the story of strengthening for instructors.

Proficient improvement arises as a focal story string in engaging teachers to help neurodiverse understudies. The story unfurls as instructors effectively participate in continuous preparation that extends how they might interpret neurodiversity, outfits them with successful showing methodologies, and cultivates an outlook that values inclusivity. This expert improvement goes past a one-time studio; it turns into a persistent excursion that adjusts to developing instructive practices, research discoveries, and the changing necessities of neurodiverse understudies inside a comprehensive system.

Understanding the different learning styles of neurodiverse understudies turns into a basic part of enabling teachers. The story investigates the fluctuated manners by which neurodiverse understudies process data, draw in with the learning climate, and express their comprehension. Separated guidance turns into a core value, permitting instructors to tailor their training techniques to oblige the different necessities of neurodiverse understudies. The story unfurls as instructors effectively look to grasp the qualities and difficulties of every understudy, making a customized approach that praises their uniqueness.

Establishing tactile well disposed conditions turns into an essential piece of enabling teachers to help neurodiverse understudies. The account investigates how teachers adjust homeroom settings, integrate tactile breaks, and give tangible devices to make comprehensive spaces where neurodiverse understudies can flourish. Strengthening includes perceiving tactile responsive qualities as well as effectively attempting to establish conditions that limit tangible over-burden and cultivate a more agreeable and helpful learning climate.

Cooperation between broad training instructors, custom curriculum instructors, support staff, and experts turns into a story subject that shapes the strengthening of teachers. The story unfurls as teachers team up to share ability, carry out separated guidance, and aggregately issue settle to meet the different advancing necessities of neurodiverse understudies. This cooperative methodology turns into a social standard that shapes the comprehensive ethos of the whole school local area, encouraging a climate where each teacher assumes a part in supporting neurodiversity.

Individualized Training Projects (IEPs) become a focal part of enabling instructors to help neurodiverse understudies. The story investigates how teachers effectively take part in the turn of events, execution, and evaluation of IEPs. Strengthening includes figuring out the substance of the IEP as well as effectively contributing experiences, perceptions, and input to guarantee its adequacy. Teachers become accomplices in the cooperative cycle, working close by guardians, subject matter experts, and care staff to make far reaching plans that address the special necessities of neurodiverse understudies.

Engaging instructors includes tending to the social difficulties neurodiverse understudies might experience inside the school climate. The story unfurls as teachers effectively take part in establishing comprehensive social conditions, carrying out interactive abilities preparing projects, and encouraging companion training drives. Strengthening stretches out to tending to harassing, advancing a culture of acknowledgment and compassion, and effectively forming a school local area where neurodiverse understudies are incorporated as well as embraced by their friends.

The story reaches out past the study hall to envelop the more extensive school local area, where teachers effectively take part in encouraging a culture of inclusivity. Engaging teachers includes establishing a school environment that values variety, challenges generalizations, and effectively advances understanding and acknowledgment. Teachers become advocates for neurodiversity inside the school, molding strategies, practices, and drives that add to a more comprehensive instructive scene.

Parental contribution turns into a basic account subject in enabling teachers to help neurodiverse understudies. The story unfurls as teachers effectively speak with guardians, looking for their experiences, grasping the qualities and difficulties of every understudy, and cooperatively attempting to establish a strong learning climate. Strengthening includes perceiving guardians as important accomplices, effectively including them in dynamic cycles, and encouraging open correspondence to guarantee an all encompassing way to deal with supporting neurodiverse understudies.

Comprehensive extracurricular exercises become a powerful part of the story, adding to the strengthening of teachers. The account investigates how instructors effectively work to guarantee that extracurricular contributions are comprehensive and open. Strengthening includes adjusting exercises, offering extra help, and cultivating a culture that energizes the support of neurodiverse understudies in sports, expressions, and other extracurricular pursuits. Instructors become advocates for inclusivity past the homeroom, effectively molding a school local area that esteems the different gifts and interests, everything being equal.

Innovation combination turns into a story string that enables teachers to help neurodiverse understudies really. The story investigates how innovation is utilized to establish comprehensive learning conditions, give elective method for correspondence, and deal customized growth opportunities. Strengthening includes instructors effectively integrating assistive innovations into their showing works on, guaranteeing that neurodiverse understudies approach devices that upgrade openness and oblige assorted learning styles.

Enabling teachers incorporates tending to the potential difficulties they might look in supporting neurodiverse understudies. The account unfurls as teachers effectively participate in self-reflection, look for extra assets and backing, and team up with partners to conquer difficulties. Proficient learning networks become an important part of strengthening, giving instructors a stage to share encounters, trade experiences, and by and large issue tackle to upgrade their capacity to help neurodiverse understudies.

The account reaches out to the more extensive schooling system, pushing for strategy changes, asset distribution, and the advancement of comprehensive practices at the foundational level. Strengthening includes instructors effectively adding to a social shift inside the instructive scene, testing foundational obstructions, and pushing for a comprehensive methodology that qualities and celebrates neurodiversity. Teachers become problem solvers inside the more extensive school system, effectively molding strategies and practices that advance inclusivity and understanding.

The effect of enabling instructors to help neurodiverse understudies reaches out past the quick school local area to add to a more extensive cultural shift. The story unfurls as alumni of schools with enabled teachers become dynamic members in the public eye, testing cultural standards, and adding to a culture that values variety and inclusivity. The examples of overcoming adversity of neurodiverse people who got support from engaged instructors become strong stories that promoter for the extension of enabling methodologies inside the more extensive instructive scene.

All in all, the story of engaging teachers to help neurodiverse understudies is an account of groundbreaking change, cooperation, and a promise to establishing instructive conditions that commend variety and cultivate inclusivity. A story perceives the critical job teachers play in forming the encounters of neurodiverse understudies and effectively adds to a social shift inside the instructive scene. As this story keeps on unfurling, it turns into an encouraging sign and a demonstration of the extraordinary force of enabled teachers in making a more impartial, sympathetic, and comprehensive society.

Chapter 5

Beyond Labels: Identity and Self-Discovery

Past Marks: Personality and Self-Disclosure

The excursion of self-disclosure and the development of character are significant parts of the human experience, rising above the limitations of cultural marks. In exploring the mind boggling landscape of personality, people leave on a mission that stretches out past the constraints forced by outside classifications. This story dives into the multi-layered elements of character and self-disclosure, investigating the nuanced exchange between private accounts, cultural assumptions, and the inborn human drive to manufacture legitimate associations with oneself as well as other people.

At the core of the investigation lies the acknowledgment that character outperforms the bounds of simple names. People are dynamic creatures, formed by a bunch of variables including individual encounters, social impacts, and inward reflections. The story unfurls as people explore the complicated course of self-revelation, stripping back the layers of cultural assumptions to uncover the bona fide self that exists past predefined classifications.

The cultural inconvenience of names turns into a focal story subject, forming the encounters of people on their excursion of self-revelation. Society frequently looks to arrange people in view of different rules like orientation, nationality, calling, or neurodiversity. These marks, while giving a similarity to arrange, can likewise limit people to foreordained assumptions and generalizations. The story investigates the effect of these marks on the arrangement of character, revealing insight into the pressure between cultural assumptions and the intrinsic human longing for self-articulation and realness.

The diversity of personality arises as a pivotal part of the story. People explore a complicated snare of converging personalities, each adding to the multi-layered embroidery of what their identity is. Factors like race, orientation, sexual direction, and financial status cross to shape interesting and converging parts of personality. The story unfurls as people embrace the lavishness of their converging characters, testing solid accounts and cultivating a more profound comprehension of the intricacies intrinsic in the human experience.

The excursion of self-disclosure is frequently set apart by thoughtfulness, a cycle through which people investigate their inward considerations, feelings, and values. This interior exchange turns into a story string that guides people towards a more significant comprehension of themselves. The account unfurls as people wrestle with inquiries of direction, meaning, and the arrangement of their genuine selves with cultural assumptions. Thoughtfulness turns into an instrument for unwinding the layers of personality, permitting people to explore the complexities of self-revelation with more noteworthy clearness.

Individual stories arise as a strong power in forming character. The accounts people tell themselves as well as other people add to the development of their own story, affecting the manner in which they see themselves and how they are seen by the world. The account investigates the job of individual narrating in self-revelation, recognizing the effect of life encounters, wins, and difficulties in molding the story of one's character. As people create and reshape their own stories, they effectively participate in the continuous course of self-revelation.

Social impacts assume a crucial part in forming character, adding to a feeling of having a place and association. The story unfurls as people explore the social scenes that illuminate their characters, embracing the practices, values, and accounts that reverberate with their genuine selves. At the same time, people might wrestle with the intricacies of social character, haggling between different social impacts and fashioning an interesting personality that mirrors the union of assorted social encounters.

The cultural assumptions set upon people become a focal story subject in the investigation of character. Society frequently forces standards, guidelines, and goals that direct the way in which people ought to act, look, and put themselves out there. The account unfurls as people face and challenge these cultural assumptions, cutting out spaces for self-appearance, realness, and the affirmation of their extraordinary personalities. The strain between cultural standards and individual realness turns into a powerful power that pushes the excursion of self-disclosure.

The idea of ease arises as a freeing force inside the story of character and self-revelation. People might encounter movements and changes in different parts of their personality, embracing the liquid idea of human life. The account unfurls as people reject the inflexibility of fixed characters, considering self-awareness, advancement, and the investigation of various features of self. Ease turns into a wellspring of strengthening, empowering people to rise above cultural assumptions and embrace the intrinsic intricacy of their characters.

Personality in the computerized age turns into a developing story subject, formed by the effect of innovation and web-based entertainment. The story investigates how online stages give spaces to self-articulation, local area building, and the investigation of different personalities. At the same time, it inspects the difficulties presented by the organized idea of online character, the strain to adjust to online patterns, and the effect of computerized communications on people's impression of self. The account unfurls as people explore the advanced scene, utilizing its true capacity for self-disclosure while fundamentally analyzing its effect on the development of personality.

The job of training in forming character turns into a story string that highlights the extraordinary force of learning conditions. Instructive establishments assume a significant part in impacting people's view of themselves as well as other people. The story investigates how comprehensive and different instructive conditions add to a more all encompassing comprehension of character, encouraging sympathy, resistance, and a festival of contrasts. Instruction turns into an impetus for self-disclosure, enabling people to explore the intricacies of personality with a receptive outlook and a widened viewpoint.

The effect of cultural assumptions on minimized and underrepresented networks turns into a strong story topic. People inside these networks frequently wrestle with the weight of generalizations, bias, and fundamental disparities that shape their personalities. The story unfurls as people inside underestimated networks state their organization, challenge cultural assumptions, and manufacture personalities that oppose the constraints forced by outside marks. The strengthening of underestimated voices turns into a strong power in reshaping the story of personality inside more extensive cultural settings.

The investigation of orientation personality and sexual direction turns into a story string that features the different manners by which people explore the intricacies of character. The story unfurls as people embrace and state their orientation personalities and sexual directions, testing cultural standards and adding to a more extensive comprehension of the ease and variety of human character. The strengthening of LGBTQ+ voices becomes essential to the story of character and self-disclosure, supporting for inclusivity, acknowledgment, and the festival of different personalities.

Neurodiversity arises as a critical story topic, testing the conventional comprehension of neurodevelopmental contrasts. The story investigates how people with different neurological profiles, like chemical imbalance, ADHD, or dyslexia, explore a world that may not necessarily comprehend or oblige their novel assets and difficulties. The story unfurls as neurodivergent people affirm their characters, advocate for acknowledgment, and effectively add to reshaping cultural view of neurodiversity. The strengthening of neurodivergent voices turns into a call for more prominent grasping, convenience, and festivity of the different manners by which human personalities work.

The job of mentorship and portrayal turns into a story subject that highlights the significance of seeing oneself reflected in others. The story unfurls as people look for tutors and good examples who share parts of their personality, giving direction, motivation, and a feeling of having a place. The strengthening of underrepresented voices as guides turns into a strong impetus for cultivating a more comprehensive and steady climate for people on their excursion of self-disclosure.

All in all, the story of character and self-disclosure is a significant and dynamic investigation of the human experience. A story rises above cultural names, embraces the intricacies of multifacetedness, and recognizes the smoothness of human character. As people explore the mind boggling embroidery of self-disclosure, the story turns into a festival of variety, a statement of legitimacy, and a strong require the strengthening of voices that have generally been underestimated or quieted. In the continuous journey for self-revelation, people produce associations with their credible selves, add to the aggregate story of human character, and effectively shape an additional comprehensive and sympathetic world.

5.1 Personal narratives of individuals on the spectrum.

Individual Stories of People on the Range: A Kaleidoscope of Encounters

The range of mental imbalance is essentially as different as the people who possess it, and inside this immense woven artwork, individual accounts arise as strong demonstrations of the rich and fluctuated encounters of those on the range.

These accounts rise above clinical portrayals, offering credible experiences into the lives, difficulties, wins, and novel viewpoints of people on the chemical imbalance range. This investigation digs into the individual stories of people on the range, winding around an embroidery that mirrors the kaleidoscope of their lives, goals, and commitments.

At the core of these individual accounts lies the affirmation of neurodiversity. The range is definitely not a solid element however a range of independence, every individual interestingly formed by their neurodevelopmental profile. These stories feature the different manners by which people on the range explore a world that may not necessarily in all cases comprehend or oblige their remarkable assets and difficulties. The lavishness of the range unfurls as private accounts challenge generalizations, dissipate confusions, and declare the worth of neurodiversity in the entirety of its aspects.

The excursion of self-disclosure arises as a conspicuous subject inside private stories of people on the range. Many describe the most common way of understanding and embracing their neurodivergent character, frequently even with cultural assumptions and winning standards. These stories mirror the significant effect of self-disclosure on people's healthy identity worth, character, and the strengthening that comes from embracing one's valid self. The excursion isn't generally straight, and individual stories offer a brief look into the dynamic and progressing interaction of self-revelation.

The difficulties looked by people on the range become account strings that wind through their own accounts. These difficulties might traverse different areas, including social cooperations, tactile awarenesses, correspondence contrasts, and exploring cultural assumptions. Individual stories give a window into the lived encounters of overseeing and defeating these difficulties, offering bits of knowledge into versatility, survival techniques, and the strength that people on the range draw from inside themselves and their networks.

Social communications and connections structure a critical part of individual stories, mirroring the intricacies and subtleties of exploring social scenes. Numerous people on the range share their encounters of shaping associations, building kinships, and developing connections. Individual stories additionally dig into the difficulties of grasping meaningful gestures, deciphering nonverbal correspondence, and the significant effect that cultural assumptions can have on friendly elements. These accounts encourage a more profound comprehension of the variety of social encounters inside the mental imbalance range.

The tactile encounters of people on the range arise as a distinctive story subject, divulging a reality where tangible upgrades might be extraordinary, overpowering, or experienced in special ways. Individual stories give firsthand records of how tactile awarenesses shape day to day existence, from the surface of textures to the murmur of bright lights. These stories additionally shed light on the versatile systems people utilize to explore tactile rich conditions, underscoring the significance of tangible inclusivity and convenience.

Training turns into a vital story string inside private stories, mirroring the differed encounters of people on the range in scholarly settings. Individual accounts investigate the effect of various instructive methodologies, the job of facilities and backing administrations, and the difficulties of exploring a school system that may not necessarily in all cases be sensitive to neurodiverse needs. These accounts advocate for comprehensive schooling, more prominent mindfulness among teachers, and the acknowledgment of the remarkable qualities that neurodivergent people bring to the learning climate.

Work and vocation ventures become basic parts of individual stories, featuring the assorted pathways that people on the range explore in the expert domain. Individual stories dig into the difficulties of new employee screenings, working environment elements, and the significance of encouraging neuroinclusive working environments. These stories additionally praise the gifts, abilities, and novel viewpoints that people on the range add to their working environments, testing assumptions and advancing the worth of variety in the labor force.

The job of family inside private stories turns into a central component, exhibiting the significant effect of familial help, understanding, and backing. Numerous people on the range relate the pivotal job their families play in their excursions, from analysis to adulthood. These stories offer looks into the elements of familial connections, the difficulties looked by guardians, kin, and more distant family individuals, and the extraordinary force of unrestricted love and acknowledgment.

Support arises as a story subject inside private stories, mirroring the dynamic job numerous people on the range take in bringing issues to light, testing generalizations, and pushing for foundational changes. Individual stories become a stage for self-promotion, enhancing voices that might have been underestimated or disregarded. These accounts add to a more extensive story of cultural change, pushing for more prominent consideration, understanding, and the destroying of boundaries that limit the chances of neurodivergent people.

Innovativeness, enthusiasm, and ability become dynamic strings inside private stories, testing the generalization of chemical imbalance as exclusively an assortment of shortages. People on the range share their interests, whether in artistic expression, sciences, innovation, or different areas, featuring the novel qualities and abilities that frequently go with neurodivergent profiles. Individual stories praise the variety of interests and commitments, encouraging a story of strengthening that goes past cultural impression of constraints.

The diversity of characters turns into a nuanced subject inside private stories, perceiving that people on the range explore a mind boggling snare of converging personalities. Individual stories mirror the assorted foundations, societies, and encounters that shape personality, accentuating the significance of perceiving and embracing the variety of a singular's character. These stories challenge one-layered depictions and add to a story that recognizes the extravagance of multifacetedness inside the chemical imbalance range.

Heartfelt and relational connections unfurl as account strings inside private stories, giving knowledge into the different ways people on the range explore the intricacies of adoration, dating, and friendship. These stories challenge generalizations encompassing connections and neurodivergence, featuring the common human encounters of association, warmth, and the quest for significant connections.

The effect of cultural insights and marks of shame turns into an intelligent subject inside private stories. Numerous people on the range share their encounters of facing misguided judgments, defeating disgrace, and effectively testing cultural mentalities towards chemical imbalance. These stories become integral assets in destroying generalizations, cultivating understanding, and making ready for a more comprehensive and tolerating society.

The significance of local area and companion support reverberates all through private stories, highlighting the job of shared encounters and a feeling of having a place. Numerous people on the range relate the extraordinary force of associating with other people who share comparative encounters, whether through help gatherings, online networks, or backing drives. These stories underscore the meaning of encouraging a feeling of local area that rises above geological limits and gives a strong organization to people on the range.

Innovation and online entertainment become essential parts of individual accounts, offering stages for self-articulation, association, and promotion. Individual stories investigate the positive and negative parts of computerized correspondence, featuring the potential for online networks to offer help, enhance voices, and encourage a feeling of having a place. These stories additionally explore the difficulties presented by online spaces, for example, cyberbullying, deception, and the organized idea of advanced characters.

The powerful idea of individual accounts mirrors the continuous advancement of individual encounters inside the mental imbalance range. These stories challenge static discernments and welcome a more profound comprehension of the ease, intricacy, and strength inborn in the existences of people on the range. As private stories keep on unfurling, they add to a more extensive story of neurodiversity — one that celebrates singularity, challenges generalizations, and supporters for an existence where each individual, paying little mind to neurodevelopmental profile, can flourish and be esteemed for their one of a kind commitments to the human experience.

5.2 Exploring the development of identity and self-advocacy.

Investigating the Improvement of Personality and Self-Promotion: An Excursion of Strengthening

The advancement of character and the development of self-support address groundbreaking excursions that people set out upon all through their lives. These interweaved processes are significantly formed by private encounters, cultural assumptions, and the advancing comprehension of one's bona fide self. This investigation dives into the complex elements of character improvement and the enabling direction of self-promotion, winding around a story that enlightens the complexities of these interconnected excursions.

Character improvement, as an idea, envelops the intricate and dynamic interaction through which people structure a feeling of what their identity is, molded by different factors like social impacts, individual encounters, connections, and cultural assumptions. This formative excursion isn't bound to a particular age or stage; rather, it unfurls across the life expectancy, constantly developing in light of inward and outer impacts. The account of personality advancement starts with the acknowledgment that people are not static creatures but rather powerful substances formed by the transaction of different components.

The beginning phases of personality improvement frequently correspond with the early stages of young life and puberty. During this period, people explore the unpredictable territory of self-revelation, slowly knowing their preferences, aversions, values, and yearnings. Family, instructive conditions, and social settings assume essential parts in molding the fundamental layers of character. The account unfurls as youthful personalities wrestle with cultural assumptions, peer impacts, and the requirement for independence, endeavoring to adjust their arising identity to the outside world.

As people progress through pre-adulthood into youthful adulthood, the investigation of character turns out to be more deliberate and nuanced. Questions encompassing profession decisions, individual convictions, and relational connections become the overwhelming focus. The story of character improvement during this stage mirrors a mission for credibility, a craving to adjust individual qualities to life decisions, and the discussion of distinction inside the more extensive social setting. The improvement of a lucid and stable character turns into an essential part of exploring the intricacies of adulthood.

Social impacts arise as a huge story string inside the formative excursion of personality. Social personality, molded by legacy, customs, language, and customs, frames a basic piece of a singular's identity. The story unfurls as people wrestle with the exchange of various social impacts, arranging the complexities of personality inside the setting of different foundations. Social personality turns into a wellspring of solidarity, versatility, and association, encouraging a more profound comprehension of the rich embroidery of human variety.

The job of connections, both familial and relational, turns into a strong part of the story of character improvement. Relational intricacies, the impact of soul mates, and the investigation of personal connections add to the developing identity. The story unfurls as people explore the intricacies of connection, partition, and the exchange among freedom and association. These connections become mirrors reflecting parts of personality, giving open doors to self-disclosure and the development of a more nuanced self-idea.

Instructive conditions, including formal and casual growth opportunities, become account impetuses inside the formative excursion of personality. Schools, universities, and learning networks offer spaces for investigation, self-articulation, and the development of assorted gifts and interests. The account unfurls as people take part chasing information, wrestle with scholastic difficulties, and explore the social elements of instructive settings. Instructive encounters add to the diverse layers of character, forming points of view, values, and goals.

The impact of cultural assumptions arises as a focal story topic inside the formative excursion of character. Cultural standards, orientation jobs, and social assumptions can apply a significant effect on how people see themselves and are seen by others. The story unfurls as people wrestle with cultural tensions, testing predefined jobs, and affirming their independence in forming their characters. The strengthening got from opposing cultural assumptions turns into a significant part of the story, cultivating a feeling of organization and validness.

The multifacetedness of personality surfaces as a dynamic and nuanced subject inside the story. People explore a complicated snare of converging personalities, including viewpoints like race, orientation, sexual direction, financial status, and neurodiversity. The story unfurls as people embrace the extravagance of their meeting personalities, testing solid accounts and encouraging a more profound comprehension of the interconnected idea of human encounters. Multifacetedness turns into a focal point through which the story of character improvement perceives and praises the variety of individual excursions.

The investigation of individual qualities and convictions turns into an essential account string inside the formative excursion of personality. As people mature, they take part in contemplation, addressing, and reflection to recognize their center standards. The account unfurls as people wrestle with moral problems, go up against moral inquiries, and expressive their convictions notwithstanding cultural standards. The improvement of a worth based character turns into a wellspring of direction, strength, and a compass for exploring life's intricacies.

The story of personality improvement reaches out into the domain of profession and work. Vocation decisions, proficient desires, and the quest for significant work become vital parts of the formative excursion. The account unfurls as people investigate their interests, explore vocation changes, and look for arrangement between private qualities and expert pursuits. The convergence of character and vocation turns into a story topic that mirrors the developing comprehension of oneself inside the setting of one's expert process.

The idea of self-promotion interweaves with the story of personality improvement, addressing a strong articulation of organization, independence, and the declaration of one's privileges and needs. Self-promotion includes the explanation of individual limits, the quest for open doors, and the dynamic commitment to dynamic cycles. The account unfurls as people explore frameworks, foundations, and cultural designs, supporting for inclusivity, equity, and the acknowledgment of different voices.

The formative direction of self-backing frequently starts with the acknowledgment of one's interesting assets, challenges, and the affirmation of individual organization. The story unfurls as people on the chemical imbalance range, for instance, effectively take part in self-backing, testing generalizations, dispersing misinterpretations, and pushing for facilities that help their different necessities. The strengthening got from self-promotion turns into a groundbreaking power inside the more extensive story of character improvement.

Schooling and mindfulness become account support points inside the formative excursion of self-promotion. People furnish themselves with information, look for data, and effectively participate in self-schooling to more readily figure out their freedoms and promoter for their necessities. The story unfurls as self-advocates become ministers for mindfulness, testing disgrace, and cultivating a more comprehensive comprehension of different characters. Training turns into a device for strengthening, empowering people to explain their remarkable points of view and add to a more educated and figuring out society.

The account of self-backing stretches out past individual excursions to include aggregate endeavors inside networks and support organizations. The force of aggregate voices becomes clear as people join to challenge foundational obstructions, advocate for strategy changes, and make spaces that perceive and celebrate different characters. The story unfurls as self-support developments add to cultural movements, advancing inclusivity, destroying biases, and cultivating a culture that esteems the independence and organization of each and every person.

The strengthening got from self-backing is reflected in the account's accentuation on the significance of self-articulation. People on the range, as well as those exploring different parts of neurodiversity, effectively share their accounts, articulate their necessities, and add to a more extensive story that challenges suppositions and advances getting it. The story unfurls as self-articulation turns into a vehicle for stalling obstructions, cultivating compassion, and making spaces that approve different encounters.

Innovation and virtual entertainment arise as account apparatuses inside the formative excursion of self-support. Online stages give spaces to people to associate, share encounters, and enhance their voices. The account unfurls as self-advocates influence advanced spaces to fabricate networks, challenge generalizations, and backer for fundamental changes. The democratization of data through innovation turns into a story subject that highlights the groundbreaking force of interconnected voices.

The convergence of character improvement and self-promotion turns into a story combination point, mirroring the interconnected idea of these excursions. People not just foster a more nuanced comprehension of their own characters yet in addition effectively advocate for the acknowledgment and festivity of different personalities inside more extensive cultural settings. The story unfurls as the individual becomes political, with individual strengthening adding to aggregate endeavors that challenge fundamental disparities, advance inclusivity, and encourage a world that esteems the intrinsic worth and respect of each and every individual.

All in all, the investigation of the improvement of personality and self-backing winds around a story embroidery that praises the extravagance, intricacy, and versatility of the human experience. It is a story of self-revelation, organization, and the statement of one's legitimate self inside the different embroidery of mankind. As people explore the unpredictable landscape of character improvement and self-backing, their accounts become indispensable strings inside a more extensive account that promoters for inclusivity, understanding, and the strengthening of each and every person to shape their own account inside the aggregate story of mankind.

5.3 The impact of societal labels and the journey towards self-acceptance.

The Effect of Cultural Names and the Excursion Towards Self-Acknowledgment: A Story of Versatility and Strengthening

Cultural names, frequently used with the expectation of characterization, convey huge load in forming individual encounters, discernments, and self-idea. This account digs into the significant effect of cultural names on people and investigates the intricate excursion towards self-acknowledgment. It is an account of flexibility, change, and the strengthening that emerges from exploring the many-sided trans-action between outer discernments and the mission for bona fide selfhood.

Cultural names, be they connected with orientation, race, neurodiversity, or different parts of personality, can go about as strong focal points through which people are seen and, thus, come to see themselves. The account starts with the acknowledgment that these names are not impartial descriptors but rather frequently convey certain suspicions, assumptions, and, on occasion, marks of shame. As people explore the cultural scene, these names become fundamental to how they are seen, affecting open doors, communications, and the actual texture of their lived encounters.

The effect of cultural marks on character improvement turns into a focal subject inside this story. From beginning phases of experience growing up to adulthood, people wrestle with the manners by which cultural assumptions shape their self-idea. The story unfurls as the heaviness of names becomes clear in molding thoughts of achievement, magnificence, knowledge, and different markers of cultural endorsement. For some, the excursion towards self-acknowledgment starts with an affirmation of the cacophony between cultural assumptions and the true self.

The focal point of neurodiversity gives a strong section point into the investigation of cultural marks and their effect. People on the chemical imbalance range, for instance, frequently experience names that outline their encounters inside a shortfall based story. The story unfurls as these people explore a world that may not necessarily comprehend or oblige their novel assets and difficulties. Cultural names add to the molding of discernments, supporting generalizations that can ruin self-acknowledgment and the more extensive cultural acknowledgment of neurodiversity.

The excursion towards self-acknowledgment includes a course of unwinding the layers of cultural assumptions and outer decisions that might have been incorporated. The story investigates the inward discourse people participate in as they face these names, testing the suppositions that have been forced upon them. It turns into a story of self-revelation, as people strip back the layers to uncover their credible selves underneath the heaviness of cultural assumptions.

Relational peculiarities, frequently a vital setting in the excursion of self-acknowledgment, become a story string inside the more extensive investigation of cultural marks. Families may accidentally propagate cultural assumptions, passing down generational standards that impact individual character advancement. The story unfurls as people explore the intricacies of familial connections, looking for acknowledgment and understanding inside the setting of the cultural marks that might have deeply impacted relational peculiarities. All the while, families can become partners in the excursion towards self-acknowledgment, offering backing and support as people rethink their feeling of character.

The effect of cultural names on emotional wellness turns into a piercing subject inside the story. Marks, particularly those connected with emotional well-being conditions, can add to shame, separation, and a feeling of distance. The story unfurls as people share their encounters of wrestling with psychological wellness marks, looking for understanding, and exploring a general public that might demonize or underestimate them. The excursion towards self-acknowledgment becomes interlaced with psychological wellness backing, testing cultural insights and encouraging compassion and backing.

Crossing personalities add layers of intricacy to the account, as people explore the convergences of race, orientation, sexuality, and different parts of character close by cultural marks. The story unfurls as people defy the extraordinary difficulties presented by different crossing marks, testing generalizations and presumptions at the convergences of their character. The excursion towards self-acknowledgment turns into a nuanced investigation of the manners by which various parts of personality meet and shape individual encounters inside the more extensive cultural setting.

Instructive conditions become essential account scenes in the investigation of cultural marks. Schools and foundations frequently assume an essential part in supporting or testing cultural assumptions. The account unfurls as people review their encounters inside instructive settings, where cultural names might impact scholastic assumptions, peer connections, and the general environment of acknowledgment or rejection. The excursion towards self-acknowledgment includes exploring these conditions, tracking down spaces for validness, and testing the impediments forced by cultural marks inside instructive settings.

The story stretches out to the domain of business, where cultural marks can shape proficient assumptions and open doors. People might experience marks connected with their profession decisions, ability, or saw reasonableness for specific jobs. The effect of these names on confidence and vocation directions turns into a story string inside the more extensive excursion towards self-acknowledgment. The account unfurls as people explore proficient scenes, testing generalizations, and supporting for acknowledgment in view of their abilities and capacities as opposed to cultural biases.

The convergence of cultural names and self-perception turns into a powerful subject inside the story. Cultural assumptions around excellence principles, weight, and actual appearance can add to body disgracing and negative self-insight. The story unfurls as people share their battles with cultural names connected with self-perception, testing ridiculous principles, and supporting for a more extensive meaning of excellence that embraces variety. The excursion towards self-acknowledgment turns into a story of recovering organization over one's body and dismissing cultural standards that sustain unsafe beliefs.

Innovation and online entertainment, while giving stages to association and self-articulation, additionally add to the propagation of cultural marks. The arranged idea of online personalities and the pervasiveness of cultural excellence guidelines in computerized spaces become story components inside the investigation of self-acknowledgment. The account unfurls as people explore the effect of web-based entertainment on their self-discernment, looking for credible associations while fighting with the potential for online spaces to support cultural names.

The strengthening got from self-support turns into a story subject inside the more extensive investigation of self-acknowledgment. People effectively challenge cultural names by standing up, sharing their accounts, and pushing for more extensive cultural comprehension. The story unfurls as self-promotion turns into an impetus for change, testing generalizations, dispersing misguided judgments, and cultivating a more comprehensive and tolerating society. The excursion towards self-acknowledgment becomes interlaced with the more extensive cultural account of testing and destroying destructive names.

The job of treatment and psychological well-being support becomes fundamental to the account of self-acknowledgment. People might look for helpful intercessions to explore the effect of cultural names on their psychological prosperity, testing incorporated convictions and encouraging a more sure self-idea. The story unfurls as treatment turns into a space for self-reflection, mending, and the improvement of survival methods to explore cultural assumptions.

The story of self-acknowledgment unfurls as a dynamic and progressing process, stressing that acknowledgment isn't an objective yet an excursion. It is a story of embracing blemishes, praising uniqueness, and testing the restrictions forced by cultural marks. The story turns into a demonstration of strength, as people explore the intricacies of cultural assumptions, defy marks that might have formed their encounters, and effectively partake in molding an additional comprehensive and tolerating cultural story.

All in all, the effect of cultural marks and the excursion towards self-acknowledgment is a story of significant importance inside the more extensive embroidery of the human experience. It is an account of people wrestling with outside assumptions, cultural standards, and the mission for legitimacy. As people explore this complex excursion, the story turns into a festival of variety, a declaration of organization, and a strong call for cultural change. It is a story of strength, strengthening, and the getting through human soul that looks for acknowledgment and understanding in a world that is continually developing.

Chapter 6

Challenges and Triumphs in Adolescence

Difficulties and Wins in Youth: Exploring the Tempest

Youthfulness, frequently portrayed as a time of tempest and stress, is a groundbreaking excursion set apart by a tornado of difficulties and wins. This story digs into the multi-layered components of youthfulness, investigating the intricacies of this significant life stage. It is an account of versatility, self-disclosure, and the victories that rise out of exploring the turbulent oceans of personality development, connections, and cultural assumptions.

The scene of pre-adulthood is painted with the brushstrokes of physical and hormonal changes that messenger the beginning of pubescence. This organic transformation, while a characteristic piece of human turn of events, acquaints young people with another domain of mindfulness and reluctance. The account unfurls as youthful people wrestle with the actual changes that reshape their bodies, exploring the landscape of mental self portrait and cultural assumptions that frequently go with the excursion through puberty.

Character development turns into a focal story subject as teenagers leave on a mission to find what their identity is and where they fit into the world. The story unfurls as people explore the many-sided course of self-revelation, investigating their qualities, convictions, and desires. Young people frequently wrestle with the pressure between cultural assumptions and the longing for independence, looking to cut out a genuine personality that lines up with their advancing identity.

The tempest of feelings that describes puberty arises as a strong story string. Hormonal variances, combined with the difficulties of self-revelation, add to a rollercoaster of feelings. The story unfurls as people explore the ups and downs of young adult feelings, wrestling with temperament swings, personality emergencies, and the extreme relational elements that mark this wild phase of life.

Peer connections become a significant part of the juvenile story. The mission for social acknowledgment and the development of companionships are focal subjects in the excursion through puberty. The account unfurls as people explore the intricacies of companion elements, defying issues of having a place, peer pressure, and the longing for social approval. The victories in this field frequently include the development of legitimate associations, the arrangement of significant companionships, and the improvement of interactive abilities that establish the groundwork for future connections.

Heartfelt and personal connections add layers of intricacy to the account of immaturity. The investigation of adoration, fascination, and the development of heartfelt associations turns into a focal topic. The account unfurls as people explore the thrilling yet testing scene of heartfelt connections, wrestling with issues of correspondence, limits, and the close to home power that goes with first loves. Wins in this field frequently include the advancement of the capacity to appreciate anyone on a deeper level, the foundation of sound relationship elements, and the development that comes from exploring the intricacies of heartfelt entrapments.

Instructive difficulties and wins become indispensable story components inside the juvenile excursion. The scholarly tensions, the journey for personality inside the instructive setting, and the quest for future objectives shape the account of puberty. The account unfurls as people explore the difficulties of scholastic assumptions, peer rivalry, and the investigation of potential profession ways. Wins in the instructive domain frequently include the improvement of flexibility, a feeling of direction, and the securing of abilities that prepare for future achievement.

Relational intricacies, while essential over the course of life, go through critical movements during puberty. The story unfurls as people explore the advancing guardian kid relationship, looking for independence while keeping up with associations with their families. Youths frequently wrestle with issues of autonomy, defiance, and the renegotiation of family jobs. Wins in the familial domain include the improvement of relational abilities, the foundation of sound limits, and the cultivating of a strong family climate that works with individual development.

Emotional well-being and prosperity arise as pivotal story topics inside the difficulties of youthfulness. The tempest of feelings, combined with cultural assumptions and scholastic tensions, can add to emotional wellness battles. The account unfurls as people face issues of nervousness, sorrow, and the shame related with looking for help. Wins in the domain of psychological well-being include the improvement of survival techniques, the development of profound flexibility, and the backing for emotional wellness mindfulness and backing inside the more extensive cultural setting.

The investigation of individual qualities, morals, and moral improvement turns into a story string inside the juvenile excursion. As people wrestle with complex moral quandaries and moral independent direction, the story unfurls as an impression of the sense of direction that directs their activities. Wins in this domain include the improvement of a solid moral establishment, moral critical thinking abilities, and a guarantee to values that add to individual trustworthiness and cultural prosperity.

The effect of cultural assumptions and social impacts turns into a strong story topic. Youths frequently fight with cultural standards, orientation assumptions, and social practices that shape their personalities. The story unfurls as people explore the strain between cultural assumptions and individual legitimacy, endeavoring to state their singularity while exploring the social scenes that illuminate their personalities. Wins in this domain include the dismissal of restricting generalizations, the festival of social variety, and the development of a solid identity inside the setting of cultural and social impacts.

Sexuality and the investigation of one's sexual personality become indispensable story components inside the young adult excursion. The story unfurls as people explore the intricacies of sexual turn of events, cultural perspectives towards sexuality, and the development of a sexual personality. Wins in this domain include the hug of one's sexual direction, the improvement of sound perspectives towards sexuality, and the encouraging of comprehensive conditions that celebrate assorted sexual characters.

The utilization of innovation and virtual entertainment turns into a cutting edge story scene inside the difficulties and wins of youth. The story unfurls as people explore the advanced domain, wrestling with issues of online character, cyberbullying, and the effect of virtual entertainment on confidence. Wins in this domain include the improvement of advanced proficiency, the development of sound web-based ways of behaving, and the formation of positive web-based networks that help the prosperity of teenagers.

The excursion through youthfulness isn't without its preliminaries, mishaps, and snapshots of vulnerability. The account unfurls as people face difficulties, endure the hardships of progress, and arise more grounded, savvier, and stronger. Wins in immaturity are much of the time the consequence of the route of these difficulties, the improvement of survival techniques, and the development of a feeling of organization that enables people to shape their own fates.

All in all, the story of difficulties and wins in youthfulness is an embroidery woven with strings of self-disclosure, flexibility, and development. It is an account of exploring the blustery oceans of personality development, connections, and cultural assumptions. As people navigate the scene of puberty, defying difficulties and celebrating wins, they arise on the opposite side with a more profound comprehension of themselves, a feeling of direction, and the versatility to confront the future with certainty. The story of immaturity is a demonstration of the extraordinary force of this phase of life, where difficulties become open doors for development, and wins become the structure blocks of a versatile and engaged adulthood.

6.1 Navigating the unique challenges of adolescence with autism.

Exploring the Special Difficulties of Puberty with Mental imbalance: An Excursion of Flexibility and Revelation

Pre-adulthood is a wild period set apart by serious self-revelation, social route, and personality development. For people on the chemical imbalance range, this excursion takes on special and frequently complicated aspects, as they explore a world that may not necessarily in all cases comprehend or oblige their neurodivergent encounters. This account dives into the unmistakable difficulties of pre-adulthood for those with mental imbalance, winding around an account of flexibility, self-support, and the victories that rise out of exploring the intricacies of this groundbreaking life stage.

The juvenile excursion starts with the acknowledgment that people on the chemical imbalance range frequently face uplifted tangible responsive qualities, making the all around extraordinary experience of youthfulness considerably seriously testing. The story unfurls as these people explore a world loaded up with tactile improvements, from clamoring lobbies to flashing glaring lights, that can be overpowering and tension initiating. The difficulties lie in dealing with these tactile contributions as well as in supporting for conditions that are tangible comprehensive and understanding.

Social communications, a focal topic of immaturity, present unpredictable difficulties for people on the chemical imbalance range. The nuanced idea of meaningful gestures, implicit principles, and the complexities of companion connections become story strings inside this excursion. The account unfurls as young people with chemical imbalance wrestle with the intricacies of shaping companionships, grasping social orders, and exploring the implicit subtleties of social elements. Wins in this domain frequently include the advancement of interactive abilities, the development of legitimate associations, and the festival of neurodiverse social encounters.

Correspondence, both verbal and non-verbal, arises as a critical story component inside the difficulties of puberty for those with mental imbalance. The account unfurls as people explore the complexities of expressive and open correspondence, confronting difficulties in deciphering non-verbal signs, mockery, and the implicit subtleties of language. Wins in this domain include the advancement of viable correspondence procedures, the hug of elective specialized techniques when required, and the festival of assorted correspondence styles that add to the extravagance of human communication.

Personality development, a focal subject of youth, takes on a novel and thoughtful quality for people on the chemical imbalance range. The story unfurls as they wrestle with inquiries of self-personality, neurodivergent pride, and the diversity of their characters inside the more extensive setting of puberty. Difficulties might emerge as people explore cultural assumptions and generalizations, looking to characterize themselves really inside the setting of their neurodivergence. Wins include the hug of neurodiverse personalities, the improvement of self-backing abilities, and the festival of the exceptional qualities that accompany being on the mental imbalance range.

Instructive conditions become multifaceted story scenes inside the difficulties of immaturity for those with mental imbalance. The story unfurls as people explore a framework that may not necessarily in every case be sensitive to their exceptional learning styles and needs. Challenges lie in pushing for facilities, grasping social elements in instructive settings, and dealing with the scholastic requests that youth brings. Wins in this domain include the advancement of self-support inside instructive settings, the acknowledgment of individual learning qualities, and the development of comprehensive instructive conditions.

The crossing point of puberty and psychological wellness turns into an impactful story subject. Teenagers with chemical imbalance might wrestle with uplifted degrees of nervousness, sadness, or the difficulties of co-happening emotional well-being conditions. The account unfurls as people explore the shame related with emotional wellness, look for help, and foster survival methods. Wins in this domain include the development of psychological wellness mindfulness, the improvement of an encouraging group of people, and the dynamic quest for procedures that advance mental prosperity.

The familial scene becomes indispensable to the story of youth for people with mental imbalance. Families might assume a pivotal part in offering help, understanding, and promotion. The account unfurls as people explore relational peculiarities, looking for both independence and association inside the familial setting. Difficulties might emerge as families figure out how to comprehend and oblige neurodivergent encounters, yet wins include the fashioning areas of strength for of bonds, the festival of neurodiverse qualities, and the dynamic job of families in cultivating versatility and self-support.

The effect of cultural discernments and disgrace turns into an intelligent topic inside the story. Young people with chemical imbalance frequently face generalizations, confusions, and the test of cultural assumptions that may not line up with their neurodivergent encounters. The story unfurls as people stand up to these cultural mentalities, challenge generalizations, and effectively take part in self-promotion to encourage a more comprehensive society. Wins include the destroying of confusions, the advancement of neurodiversity mindfulness, and the dynamic job of people in forming cultural accounts.

The domain of work and future goals adds one more layer to the account of pre-adulthood for people with mental imbalance. The difficulties might include exploring cultural assumptions about profession ways, new employee screenings, and work environment elements. The account unfurls as people investigate their interests, gifts, and profession desires, looking for pathways that line up with their assets. Wins in this domain include the festival of neurodiverse commitments in the labor force, the advancement of comprehensive business rehearses, and the dynamic quest for satisfying and significant vocation ways.

Innovation and virtual entertainment become account instruments inside the difficulties of puberty for those with chemical imbalance. The account unfurls as people draw in with advanced spaces, exploring the potential for both positive and pessimistic encounters on the web. Wins include utilizing innovation for self-articulation, backing, and local area working, while additionally effectively tending to the difficulties presented by cyberbullying, falsehood, and the arranged idea of advanced characters.

The convergence of youth, orientation character, and sexual direction adds intricacy to the story for people with mental imbalance. The difficulties include exploring cultural assumptions, understanding and communicating orientation character, and shaping heartfelt connections. The story unfurls as people explore these intricacies, looking for acknowledgment and understanding inside the crossing point of neurodivergence and various personalities. Wins include the festival of LGBTQ+ personalities, the advancement of comprehensive spaces, and the acknowledgment of the different manners by which people on the chemical imbalance range insight and express their orientation and sexuality.

Self-promotion turns into a strong story subject inside the difficulties of puberty for those with chemical imbalance. The story unfurls as people effectively take part in self-promotion, declaring their requirements, testing cultural perspectives, and cultivating a feeling of organization. Wins in this domain include the advancement of self-backing abilities, the formation of steady organizations, and the commitment of people to the more extensive support endeavors that advance neurodiversity and inclusivity.

All in all, the story of exploring the extraordinary difficulties of pre-adulthood with mental imbalance is a demonstration of the versatility, strength, and variety of people on the mental imbalance range. It is an account of self-revelation, promotion, and wins that rise up out of exploring the intricacies of puberty inside the setting of neurodivergence.

As these people navigate the scene of youth, they add to a more extensive story that calls for figuring out, acknowledgment, and the festival of different personalities. The excursion turns into a demonstration of the groundbreaking force of self-support, strength, and the persevering through soul that pushes people with chemical imbalance towards an eventual fate of strengthening, acknowledgment, and significant association.

6.2 Social dynamics, peer relationships, and self-esteem.

Social Elements, Friend Connections, and Confidence: Exploring the Complicated Interchange

The many-sided dance of social elements and friend connections during different phases of life assumes a urgent part in molding one's confidence, impacting personality development, and adding to generally prosperity. This story digs into the perplexing transaction between friendly elements, peer connections, and confidence, investigating the nuanced manners by which these components combine and effect individual encounters.

Social Elements as the Embroidery of Cooperation

Social elements comprise the many-sided trap of cooperations that people take part in inside their social surroundings. From youth to puberty and then some, these elements shape and are molded by the social, cultural, and relational settings in which people track down themselves. At the center of social elements lies the basic human requirement for association and having a place, pushing people to explore the perplexing territory of connections to satisfy this natural longing.

The story starts with the acknowledgment that social elements are diverse, incorporating a range of collaborations going from short lived experiences to profound, significant connections. It unfurls as people gain proficiency with the implicit principles of social commitment, translate the subtleties of non-verbal correspondence, and explore the recurring pattern of overall vibes. Social elements, basically, become the scenery against which the show of friend connections and the advancement of confidence unfurls.

Peer Connections: Exploring the Social Scene

Peer connections arise as focal heroes in the account of social elements. From youth companionships to juvenile factions and grown-up groups of friends, the idea of friend associations fundamentally impacts a singular's identity and having a place. The account unfurls as people explore the difficulties and wins of shaping, keeping up with, and once in a while growing out of these essential social bonds.

Youth fellowships, set apart by shared interests and the straightforwardness of play, establish the groundwork for the perplexing woven artwork of friend connections. The story investigates the delight of brotherhood, the aggravation of contentions, and the persevering through effect of young life kinships on the advancement of interactive abilities and early confidence. As people change to youth, the scene of friend connections turns out to be more complicated, set apart by the investigation of character, the development of coteries, and the mission for social acknowledgment.

Youthfulness, a pot of character development, strengthens the meaning of friend connections. The account digs into the profound power of high school companionships, the effect of friend pressure, and the investigation of close connections. People explore the fragile equilibrium of fitting in while attesting their special characters, confronting both the elevating backing of dear fellowships and the possible entanglements of social rejection or harassing. The advancement of confidence turns out to be unpredictably weaved with the triumphs and difficulties experienced inside the domain of companion connections during this groundbreaking phase of life.

In adulthood, the story advances as friend connections take on different structures, going from proficient organizations to picked families. The intricacies of exploring working environment elements, shaping profound associations, and dealing with the advancing scene of fellowships become fundamental components of the account. People wrestle with the equilibrium of individual and expert connections, confronting the difficulties of keeping up with social associations in the midst of the requests of adulthood.

The Effect of Friend Connections on Confidence

At the core of the account lies the significant effect of friend connections on confidence, the evaluative focal point through which people see their own value and abilities. Peer connections act as mirrors reflecting back parts of oneself, impacting one's self-idea, and adding to the improvement of confidence. The account unfurls as people incorporate the input, both positive and pessimistic, got from peers, forming their impression of capability, agreeability, and in general self-esteem.

During youth, positive companion connections and strong kinships add to the improvement of a solid confidence establishment. The story investigates the delight of shared play, the fellowship of companionships, and the feeling of having a place inside a friend bunch. On the other hand, encounters of dismissal, prohibition, or tormenting can create shaded areas on confidence, making difficulties that people might convey into pre-adulthood and adulthood.

Pre-adulthood enhances the stakes of friend connections on confidence. The story dives into the mission for social acknowledgment, the effect of cultural excellence norms, and the development of close connections as compelling variables in molding confidence during this weak period. Positive companion approval can encourage a feeling of certainty and self-esteem, while encounters of dismissal or social estrangement might prompt a pessimistic effect on confidence, possibly adding to psychological well-being difficulties.

In adulthood, the story grows to envelop the changed features of confidence impacted by the intricacy of grown-up peer connections. Working environment elements, groups of friends, and heartfelt organizations become urgent fields where confidence is consistently formed and tried. People explore the difficulties of correlation, an inability to acknowledge success, and the quest for approval inside the multifaceted trap of grown-up connections.

Exploring Difficulties: Friend Strain, Social Prohibition, and Tormenting

Challenges inside the scene of friend connections arise as huge story strings. Peer pressure, the strong power applied by normal practices and assumptions inside a friend bunch, turns into a focal subject. The account unfurls as people wrestle with the pressure among congruity and uniqueness, confronting decisions that may either reinforce or subvert their confidence. Wins include the capacity to oppose negative companion pressure, state individual qualities, and develop areas of strength for an of self-esteem that rises above outside impacts.

Social rejection and harassing, tragically common in different phases of life, add intricacy to the story. The effect of being shunned or exposed to harassing turns into a piercing subject. The account investigates the profound cost of avoidance, the scars left by harassing encounters, and the flexibility expected to defeat these difficulties. Wins lie in the capacity to explore misfortune, look for help, and develop an interior locus of approval that fills in as a cradle against outside cynicism.

Developing Sound Friend Connections: Correspondence, Compassion, and Limits

Inside the story, the excursion towards developing sound friend connections turns into a core value. Compelling correspondence, the capacity to communicate one's thoughts truly and compassionately, arises as a urgent expertise. The story unfurls as people explore the intricacies of correspondence, figuring out how to express their requirements, pay attention to other people, and encourage shared grasping inside the domain of friend connections.

Compassion turns into a groundbreaking power inside the story, permitting people to comprehend and reverberate with the encounters of their friends. The development of sympathy adds to the improvement of empathetic and strong companion connections. The story investigates the force of compassion in establishing a positive social climate that sustains confidence and encourages a feeling of having a place.

Laying out and keeping up with limits inside peer connections become fundamental parts of the account. The capacity to state limits, express private cutoff points, and regard the limits of others adds to the making of sound and deferential social elements. The story unfurls as people explore the fragile equilibrium between closeness and independence, perceiving that defining and regarding limits is fundamental for the support of positive companion connections and the conservation of confidence.

The Job of Computerized Spaces: Innovation, Online Entertainment, and Confidence

In the contemporary story, the job of computerized spaces, formed by innovation and online entertainment, turns into a critical scene inside the elements of friend connections. The story unfurls as people explore the effect of online connections on confidence, perceiving the potential for both positive and pessimistic impacts inside the advanced domain. The arranged idea of online characters, the commonness of social examination, and the potential for cyberbullying become account components inside the investigation of the computerized element of friend connections.

Wins inside this domain include utilizing computerized spaces for positive self-articulation, building strong web-based networks, and effectively dealing with one's advanced impression to defend confidence. The story mirrors the advancing idea of companion connections in the computerized age, where people should explore the intricacies of online elements while safeguarding their psychological and profound prosperity.

Developing Strength and Self-Approval

The story finishes up with a reflection on the development of versatility and self-approval as fundamental components in exploring the unpredictable exchange of social elements, peer connections, and confidence. Flexibility, the capacity to return from difficulties, turns into a story subject as people face mishaps inside peer connections. The account unfurls as people draw upon their internal strength, look for help, and foster survival techniques that reinforce their ability to explore the inescapable highs and lows of social collaborations.

Self-approval arises as an extraordinary victory inside the story. The capacity to determine a feeling of worth from interior sources as opposed to depending exclusively on outside approval turns into a foundation of sound confidence. The story investigates the excursion towards self-acknowledgment, confidence, and the acknowledgment that one's inborn worth goes past the decisions of companions or cultural assumptions.

All in all, the story of social elements, peer connections, and confidence winds around an embroidery of interconnected encounters that shape the human excursion. It is an account of exploring the complicated exchange between individual character and the social mirrors reflected according to peers. As people cross the scenes of life as a youngster, pre-adulthood, and adulthood, the story mirrors the difficulties, wins, and extraordinary power inserted inside the fragile dance of social elements, peer connections, and the improvement of confidence. A story calls for sympathy, versatility, and the persistent quest for self-approval in the steadily developing embroidery of human association.

6.3 Success stories of individuals overcoming obstacles during this stage.

Examples of overcoming adversity of People Conquering Impediments: Wins In the midst of Difficulties

In the fantastic embroidered artwork of human life, certain accounts sparkle splendidly as guides of motivation and versatility. The narratives of people beating impressive obstructions during different phases of life stand as demonstration of the unyielding human soul. This account dives into the complexities of examples of overcoming adversity, investigating the excursions of people who, despite everything, arose victorious during urgent phases of their lives.

Adolescence Wins: Exploring Difficulty with Boldness

The excursion frequently starts in adolescence, where the seeds of strength are planted in the midst of difficulty. Kids confronting difficulties, for example, learning handicaps, medical problems, or financial difficulties show striking strength in their capacity to beat obstructions. The story unfurls as these youthful people explore the instructive scene, conquering scholastic obstacles and cultural assumptions.

Consider the narrative of Emily, a kid with dyslexia who changed her battle into an excursion of win. Notwithstanding confronting hardships in customary learning conditions, Emily found her own one of a kind approach to engrossing information. With the backing of devoted teachers and a sustaining home climate, she vanquished her learning difficulties as well as arisen as an imaginative scholar, utilizing her extraordinary viewpoint to succeed in regions past scholastics.

Juvenile Flexibility: Confronting Character Difficulties with Elegance

The juvenile stage, set apart by extraordinary self-disclosure and social elements, presents its own arrangement of deterrents. People wrestling with issues connected with personality, self-perception, or cultural assumptions grandstand wonderful versatility during this extraordinary period. The story investigates accounts of teens who confronted harassing, cultural tensions, or psychological wellness challenges, yet arose with a fortified identity.

Meet Alex, a juvenile exploring the intricacies of orientation personality in a general public wrestling with assumptions. Regardless of confronting separation and misconception, Alex turned into a vocal backer for LGBTQ+ freedoms. The story unfurls as Alex embraced their own way of life as well as prepared for others to do likewise, testing cultural standards and encouraging a more comprehensive climate for all.

Youthful Grown-up Wins: Producing Ways Past Assumptions

As people change into youthful adulthood, the difficulties frequently strengthen, including instructive pursuits, vocation goals, and the mission for freedom. Examples of overcoming adversity inside this stage are set apart by strength notwithstanding difficulties, assurance to overcome cultural presumption, and the capacity to cut novel ways regardless of foundational boundaries.

Consider the story of James, a youthful grown-up with an actual handicap, who confronted suspicion about his capacity to seek after a requesting profession in designing. Courageous, James procured his science certificate as well as turned into a pioneer in supporting for open foundation. His story unfurls as a demonstration of the force of assurance, testing suppositions, and producing ways that go past cultural assumptions.

Proficient Victories: Breaking Boundaries in the Working environment

The expert domain frequently turns into a landmark where people defy impediments connected with orientation, race, handicap, or other cultural predispositions. Examples of overcoming adversity inside this space exhibit people who got through biased based impediments as well as made ready for additional comprehensive and various working environments.

Enter Maria, an expert exploring the difficulties of being the main lady in a male-overwhelmed industry. Maria's story unfurls as she succeeds in her vocation as well as turns into a backer for orientation variety in her field. Her story turns into a guide for other people, showing the force of persistence and the effect of separating foundational obstructions inside the expert scene.

Exploring Emotional wellness Difficulties: Accounts of Versatility and Recuperation

The account of conquering deterrents would be deficient without recognizing the victories of those confronting psychological well-being difficulties. People who explore conditions like gloom, tension, or injury exhibit extraordinary strength in their excursion towards mending and recuperation.

Take the narrative of Carlos, who confronted the murkiness of wretchedness however arisen with a freshly discovered appreciation for emotional well-being promotion. Carlos' story unfurls as he not just looks for treatment for his own prosperity yet in addition turns into a vocal ally, breaking the shame encompassing emotional wellness and empowering others to look for help. His process turns into a demonstration of the groundbreaking force of strength and the significance of cultivating a steady local area around psychological well-being.

Nurturing Wins: Sustaining Versatile Fates

For guardians confronting the difficulties of bringing up kids with one of a kind requirements or medical issue, the excursion turns into an embroidery of wins entwined with affection and devotion. The story investigates accounts of guardians who, with faithful responsibility, give an underpinning of help to their youngsters to defeat hindrances and prosper.

Consider the story of Sarah, a mother supporting for her kid with chemical imbalance. Sarah's story unfurls as she explores the intricacies of the schooling system, advocates for comprehensive conditions, and commends her youngster's exceptional assets. Her process turns into a motivation for different guardians, outlining the force of support, love, and strength in sustaining the capability of each and every youngster.

Old Flexibility: Tracking down Strength in Later Years

As people cross the later phases of life, the account of conquering snags keeps on developing. Accounts of old people finding versatility even with wellbeing difficulties, misfortune, or cultural impression of maturing feature the getting through soul that challenges age-related generalizations.

Meet Henry, an old honorable man confronting the difficulties of versatility issues. Henry's story unfurls as he adjusts to his changing conditions as well as turns into a supporter for openness in broad daylight spaces. His story turns into a demonstration of the strength found in later years and difficulties the thought that age decreases one's ability for significant commitments to society.

Social Victories: Saving Legacy In the midst of Misfortune

Inside the rich woven artwork of social variety, examples of overcoming adversity arise as people beat obstructions connected with segregation, removal, or the disintegration of social legacy. The account investigates accounts of people who, in the midst of cultural difficulties, safeguard and commend their social personality, adding to the lively mosaic of human encounters.

Consider the tale of Aisha, who confronted segregation as a migrant yet arisen as a social minister, advancing comprehension and appreciation for her legacy. Aisha's story unfurls as she safeguards her social roots as well as cultivates a feeling of solidarity and acknowledgment inside her local area. Her story turns into a festival of social victories that rise above misfortune.

Wins Notwithstanding Wellbeing Difficulties: Accounts of Recuperating and Trust

The story of defeating obstructions frequently crosses with the domain of wellbeing challenges. People confronting persistent sicknesses, incapacities, or life changing ailments exhibit amazing versatility, transforming their accounts into encouraging signs for others exploring comparative excursions.

Meet David, who stood up to a life changing conclusion with mental fortitude and assurance. David's account unfurls as he goes through thorough clinical medicines as well as turns into a supporter for examination and mindfulness. His story turns into an image of trust, showing that even notwithstanding wellbeing challenges, people can track down strength, reason, and the ability to rouse others with their flexibility.

The Consistent ideas: Flexibility, Assurance, and Local area Backing

Across these assorted accounts, consistent ideas of strength, assurance, and the crucial job of local area support arise. The victories inside these accounts are not singular undertakings but rather aggregate accomplishments energized by the help of friends and family, coaches, and networks that assembly around people confronting hindrances. The story highlights the significance of encouraging conditions that elevate, engage, and perceive the innate worth and possible inside each person.

All in all, the examples of overcoming adversity of people conquering impediments structure a rich embroidery of human encounters, woven with strings of versatility, assurance, and the groundbreaking influence of the human soul. These stories rise above unambiguous difficulties, addressing the all inclusive ability to defeat misfortune and arise more grounded, smarter, and more merciful. They become wellsprings of motivation as well as tokens of the limitless possible inside every person to win over impediments and add to the aggregate account of human flexibility.

Chapter 7

Transitioning to Adulthood

The excursion from youth to adulthood is a groundbreaking odyssey, set apart by a heap of difficulties, wins, and the unfurling of individual personality. This story digs into the mind boggling embroidery of changing to adulthood, investigating the multi-layered parts of this critical stage in human turn of events. From the complexities of personality development to the difficulties of freedom, the story unfurls as a reflection on the unknown waters explored by people as they set out on the excursion to adulthood.

Personality Arrangement: The Journey for Self-Revelation

At the core of the change to adulthood lies the significant mission for personality development. The story starts with the acknowledgment that youthfulness fills in as a pot where people wrestle with inquiries of self-personality, reason, and their position on the planet. This excursion unfurls as youthful grown-ups investigate their qualities, convictions, and yearnings, trying to cut out a real personality that lines up with their advancing identity.

The intricacies of character development become obvious as people explore the interaction between cultural assumptions, familial impacts, and individual desires. The account investigates how social foundations, orientation personality, and financial elements shape the focal point through which people view themselves. Wins in this domain frequently include the hug of different characters, the dismissal of restricting generalizations, and the development of a solid identity that rises above outside assumptions.

Instructive Pursuits: Exploring The scholarly world and Vocation Yearnings

The change to adulthood is entwined with the quest for training and the investigation of profession ways. The story unfurls as people explore the difficulties of scholarly assumptions, vocation decisions, and the developing scene of expert yearnings. The strain to come to urgent conclusions about advanced education and future professions turns into a focal subject, as youthful grown-ups wrestle with the harmony among energy and reasonableness.

Consider the narrative of Maya, a youthful grown-up exploring the perplexing decisions of chasing after a vocation lined up with her energy for human expressions while likewise thinking about functional contemplations. Maya's story becomes meaningful of the more extensive difficulties looked by a larger number of people as they explore the instructive and vocation scenes. Wins in this domain include the arrangement of individual interests with proficient pursuits, the quest for deep rooted learning, and the acknowledgment that outcome in adulthood envelops a range of satisfying ways.

Freedom and Independence: Building Starting points for Adulthood

One of the characterizing elements of changing to adulthood is the mission for freedom and independence. The story investigates how youthful grown-ups explore the change from reliance on familial designs to laying out their own establishments. The difficulties of monetary obligation, dynamic independence, and the quest for individual objectives become fundamental components of this excursion.

Consider the story of James, who passed on his old neighborhood to seek after advanced education in an alternate city. James' story unfurls as he wrestles with the difficulties of living freely, overseeing funds, and settling on choices that shape his future. The story mirrors the more extensive topic of youthful grown-ups fashioning their ways, beating difficulties, and laying the preparation for an independent adulthood. Wins in this domain include the advancement of fundamental abilities, monetary education, and the development of strength despite the recently discovered liabilities that accompany freedom.

Exploring Connections: From Kinships to Heartfelt Bonds

The scene of connections goes through a change during the progress to adulthood. The story investigates how youthful grown-ups explore the intricacies of fellowships, heartfelt connections, and the advancing elements with family. The difficulties of shaping significant associations, overseeing clashes, and laying out solid limits become pivotal story strings inside this domain.

Consider the tale of Emma, who explores the difficulties of keeping up with kinships while seeking after a requesting vocation. Emma's story turns into an impression of the difficult exercise numerous youthful grown-ups face as they endeavor to sustain connections in the midst of the requests of adulthood. Wins in this domain include the development of the capacity to understand people on a profound level, the arrangement of valid associations, and the acknowledgment that connections add to the embroidery of a satisfying grown-up life.

Psychological wellness and Prosperity: Exploring the Profound Scene

The profound scene turns into a powerful story topic as youthful grown-ups wrestle with the intricacies of psychological well-being and prosperity. The account unfurls as people explore pressure, uneasiness, and the cultural assumptions that can add to personal difficulties. The acknowledgment of psychological wellness as an indispensable part of generally prosperity turns into a groundbreaking component inside the story.

Consider the tale of Alex, who defies the disgrace encompassing emotional wellness and effectively looks for help during testing times. Alex's story mirrors the more extensive excursion of numerous youthful grown-ups in recognizing the significance of emotional well-being, looking for help when required, and encouraging a culture of transparency around profound prosperity. Wins in this domain include the improvement of survival techniques, the development of strength, and the support for emotional wellness mindfulness inside the more extensive cultural setting.

Social and Cultural Assumptions: Exploring Complex Real factors

The story recognizes the effect of social and cultural assumptions on the progress to adulthood. Youthful grown-ups frequently wind up exploring the pressure between conventional assumptions and the craving for individual independence. The account unfurls as people defy generalizations, challenge cultural standards, and declare their characters inside different social settings.

Consider the story of Raj, who explores the assumptions put on him inside a social system that esteems specific vocation ways over others. Raj's story becomes meaningful of the more extensive difficulties looked by youthful grown-ups as they explore the crossing point of social practices and individual desires. Wins in this domain include the festival of different personalities, the dismissal of restricting generalizations, and the encouraging of comprehensive conditions that honor individual decisions.

Exploring Computerized Spaces: Innovation, Virtual Entertainment, and Mental self portrait

In the contemporary account, the job of computerized spaces becomes vital to the progress to adulthood. The story investigates how youthful grown-ups explore the effect of innovation and virtual entertainment on mental self view, connections, and cultural assumptions. The arranged idea of online personalities, the predominance of social correlation, and the potential for cyberbullying become huge components inside this advancing scene.

Consider the tale of Mia, who effectively deals with her computerized presence to cultivate a solid mental self portrait and credible associations. Mia's account mirrors the more extensive subject of youthful grown-ups utilizing advanced spaces for positive self-articulation while effectively tending to the difficulties presented by the arranged idea of online personalities. Wins in this domain include computerized proficiency, the development of positive web-based networks, and the acknowledgment of the expected effect of advanced spaces on mental and profound prosperity.

Parental and Familial Elements: Exploring Advancing Connections

The change to adulthood includes a reconfiguration of familial elements, as youthful grown-ups declare their freedom while keeping up with associations with their families. The story investigates the difficulties and wins of exploring developing associations with guardians and kin, perceiving the moving jobs and obligations inside the family structure.

Consider the narrative of Olivia, who wrestles with the equilibrium of stating her freedom while keeping a cozy relationship with her loved ones. Olivia's story turns into an impression of the more extensive subject of youthful grown-ups exploring the intricacies of familial elements during the progress to adulthood. Wins in this domain include open correspondence, common comprehension, and the acknowledgment of the advancing idea of family connections.

Difficulties and Wins in Vocation Pursuits: Exploring the Expert Scene

The expert domain turns into a focal story scene as youthful grown-ups leave on vocation pursuits. The account unfurls as people explore the difficulties of entering the labor force, seeking after vocation objectives, and dealing with the harmony between proficient desires and individual satisfaction. The assumptions, misfortunes, and wins inside the expert scene become essential parts of the progress to adulthood.

Consider the story of Chris, who defies the difficulties of a cutthroat work market while remaining consistent with his enthusiasm for social effect. Chris' story mirrors the more extensive topic of youthful grown-ups exploring the intricacies of vocation pursuits, settling on decisions that line up with their qualities, and tracking down satisfaction inside the expert scene. Wins in this domain include tirelessness, flexibility, and the acknowledgment that progress in adulthood envelops an all encompassing perspective on expert and individual prosperity.

Monetary Proficiency: Exploring the Financial Real factors

The monetary real factors of adulthood deliver the difficulties of monetary obligation and education. The story investigates how youthful grown-ups explore planning, monetary preparation, and the more extensive financial scene. The capacity to oversee funds, pursue informed choices, and plan for what's to come turns into a focal subject inside this story string.

Consider the tale of Ryan, who effectively instructs himself on monetary proficiency and arrives at informed conclusions about saving and financial planning. Ryan's account becomes significant of the more extensive subject of youthful grown-ups exploring the financial real factors of adulthood with strength and pre-science. Wins in this domain include monetary schooling, dependable navigation, and the acknowledgment of the significance of long haul monetary preparation.

Local area Commitment: Exploring Social Obligation

As youthful grown-ups progress to adulthood, the story investigates the job of local area commitment and social obligation. The quest for significant commitments to society, promotion for social issues, and the acknowledgment of one's job inside the more extensive local area become necessary parts of this excursion.

Consider the tale of Maya, who effectively participates in humanitarian effort and social support to add to positive change. Maya's story mirrors the more extensive subject of youthful grown-ups perceiving their organization in molding a superior world and effectively adding to local area prosperity.

Wins in this domain include the development of a feeling of social obligation, promotion for good change, and the acknowledgment of the interconnectedness of individual activities with more extensive cultural effects.

The Continuum of Picking up: Exploring Deep rooted Development

The story finishes up with the acknowledgment that the progress to adulthood is definitely not a limited endpoint yet rather a continuum of learning and development. The excursion includes a guarantee to deep rooted learning, self-improvement, and the acknowledgment that adulthood is a dynamic and developing phase of life.

Consider the account of Elena, who effectively looks for potential open doors for ceaseless learning and self-awareness. Elena's account becomes significant of the more extensive subject of youthful grown-ups perceiving the significance of continuous personal growth and the quest for information all through their lives. Wins in this domain include a promise to self-improvement, versatility, and the acknowledgment that the excursion of progressing to adulthood is a continuous course of disclosure.

All in all, the story of changing to adulthood unfurls as a complicated, diverse excursion enveloping character development, instructive pursuits, freedom, connections, psychological well-being, social elements, computerized spaces, familial associations, profession pursuits, monetary proficiency, local area commitment, and the continuum of learning. A story mirrors the flexibility, difficulties, and wins experienced by youthful grown-ups as they explore the unfamiliar waters of adulthood, producing ways that are particularly their own. As these people leave on the excursion of self-disclosure and development, they add to the aggregate story of transitioning into the intricacies and conceivable outcomes of adulthood.

7.1 Challenges and opportunities for individuals with autism entering adulthood.

Difficulties and Amazing open doors for People with Chemical imbalance Entering Adulthood: Exploring the Change

The progress from youth to adulthood is a mind boggling venture for any individual, set apart by a bunch of difficulties and open doors. Notwithstanding, for people with chemical imbalance, this progress conveys extraordinary contemplations that require a nuanced comprehension of their assets, needs, and the cultural elements that shape their way. This story investigates the difficulties and valuable open doors looked by people with chemical imbalance as they explore the change into adulthood, revealing insight into the intricacies of this excursion and the potential for significant open doors that add to a more comprehensive society.

Challenges in Schooling and Business: Opening Potential

One of the essential difficulties looked by people with mental imbalance entering adulthood lies in the domains of schooling and business. The conventional designs of training and the labor force may not necessarily in every case line up with the exceptional qualities and learning styles of people on the chemical imbalance range. The story unfurls as these people explore the difficulties of instructive facilities, social coordination, and the quest for significant business open doors.

Consider the narrative of Alex, a youthful grown-up with mental imbalance, who confronted challenges in the standard schooling system yet found an enthusiasm for innovation. Alex's story mirrors the more extensive difficulties looked by people with chemical imbalance in finding instructive conditions that take care of their particular necessities and qualities. Wins in this domain include the acknowledgment and execution of comprehensive instructive practices, custom-made emotionally supportive networks, and the opening of the undiscovered expected that people with chemical imbalance frequently have in fields like innovation, expressions, and sciences.

Social Elements and Connections: Exploring the Relational Scene

One more critical part of the progress to adulthood for people with chemical imbalance includes exploring the complex scene of social elements and connections. Challenges in friendly correspondence, figuring out expressive gestures, and shaping associations might be more articulated, adding to sensations of seclusion and avoidance. The story unfurls as people with mental imbalance endeavor to lay out significant associations, encouraging kinships, and exploring the intricacies of heartfelt connections.

Consider the tale of Emma, a young lady with chemical imbalance who confronted difficulties in framing companionships during her school years. Emma's story becomes meaningful of the more extensive social difficulties people with mental imbalance might experience, featuring the significance of encouraging figuring out, compassion, and establishing comprehensive social conditions. Wins in this domain include the advancement of neurodiversity mindfulness, the development of interactive abilities through designated mediations, and the acknowledgment of the special viewpoints and qualities that people with mental imbalance bring to connections.

Free Living and Fundamental abilities: Building an Establishment for Independence

Freedom and the authority of fundamental abilities are critical parts of the change to adulthood for people with chemical imbalance. The difficulties in creating functional abilities for day to day living, overseeing individual budgets, and exploring public spaces autonomously can be huge. The story unfurls as people pursue fabricating an establishment for independence, beating obstructions to free living, and taking part effectively in their networks.

Consider the tale of James, a youthful grown-up with chemical imbalance, who left on an excursion to master fundamental abilities, for example, cooking, shopping for food, and utilizing public transportation. James' story turns into a portrayal of the more extensive difficulties and wins in encouraging freedom for people with mental imbalance, underscoring the significance of custom fitted emotionally supportive networks, professional preparation, and local area drives that advance comprehensive living. Open doors in this domain include the advancement of professional preparation programs, upheld living courses of action, and local area based drives that enable people with chemical imbalance to lead satisfying, autonomous lives.

Psychological wellness and Prosperity: Exploring the Close to home Scene

The change to adulthood delivers contemplations for psychological well-being and prosperity that are necessary to the general excursion of people with chemical imbalance. Challenges in overseeing tension, tactile awarenesses, and adjusting to changing conditions might affect the profound scene altogether. The story unfurls as people with chemical imbalance, alongside their families and encouraging groups of people, explore the intricacies of emotional well-being, cultivating versatility and prosperity.

Consider the narrative of Sarah, a young lady with chemical imbalance, who effectively takes part in remedial exercises to oversee uneasiness and stress. Sarah's story mirrors the more extensive subject of focusing on psychological wellness for people with chemical imbalance, underscoring the significance of open emotional well-being administrations, tactile cordial spaces, and an all encompassing way to deal with prosperity. Wins in this domain include destigmatizing psychological well-being conversations, advancing self-backing, and establishing strong conditions that perceive and oblige the one of a kind feelings of people with mental imbalance.

Legitimate and Backing Difficulties: Guaranteeing Privileges and Incorporation

The progress to adulthood for people with mental imbalance frequently includes exploring lawful and promotion difficulties to guarantee their freedoms and incorporation inside society. Admittance to suitable facilities, work valuable open doors, and local area commitment might be hindered by foundational boundaries. The story unfurls as people, families, and supporters pursue destroying these obstructions, upholding for strategy changes, and advancing comprehensive practices.

Consider the narrative of David, a youthful grown-up with chemical imbalance, who confronted difficulties in getting to sensible facilities in his work environment. David's account mirrors the more extensive legitimate and support difficulties people with mental imbalance might experience, featuring the requirement for regulative measures that shield their freedoms.

Wins in this domain include the dynamic contribution of backing gatherings, lawful changes that address segregation, and the production of comprehensive strategies that advance equivalent open doors for people with chemical imbalance.

Monetary Autonomy and Financial Open doors: Exploring the Financial Scene

Getting monetary freedom and significant financial open doors is a basic part of the progress to adulthood for people with chemical imbalance. Difficulties might emerge in getting to professional preparation, finding work that lines up with their abilities, and accomplishing monetary strength. The story unfurls as people with mental imbalance, alongside managers and policymakers, pursue setting out financial open doors that perceive and esteem neurodiversity.

Consider the narrative of Mia, a youthful grown-up with mental imbalance, who sought after her enthusiasm for craftsmanship and transformed it into an independent company. Mia's story turns into a portrayal of the pioneering soul inside the chemical imbalance local area, underscoring the potential for monetary strengthening through different work models. Wins in this domain include cultivating comprehensive working environments, supporting business venture drives, and making monetary designs that focus on the qualities and commitments of people with mental imbalance.

Post-Auxiliary Training: Growing Access and Incorporation

Admittance to post-optional schooling is a critical thought for people with chemical imbalance entering adulthood. Challenges in exploring school conditions, getting to fitting facilities, and cultivating a strong instructive culture might influence their quest for advanced education. The story unfurls as instructive foundations, close by people with mental imbalance and their encouraging groups of people, pursue extending access and advancing incorporation.

Consider the tale of Chris, a youthful grown-up with chemical imbalance, who confronted difficulties in getting to comprehensive instructive conditions during his school years. Chris' account mirrors the more extensive difficulties inside the post-auxiliary schooling system, featuring the significance of comprehensive practices, tangible well disposed spaces, and backing administrations that take special care of the assorted necessities of understudies with mental imbalance. Wins in this domain include the advancement of neurodiversity inside instructive settings, the execution of comprehensive educational programs, and the formation of steady grounds conditions.

Local area Commitment and Social Incorporation: Building Associations

Dynamic support in local area life and social consideration is an essential part of the progress to adulthood for people with mental imbalance. Difficulties might emerge in getting to local area spaces, taking part in friendly exercises, and encouraging associations with peers. The story unfurls as people, local area pioneers, and associations make progress toward making comprehensive spaces, advancing get-togethers that oblige different necessities, and cultivating a feeling of having a place.

Consider the tale of Maya, a young lady with mental imbalance, who effectively takes part in local area occasions and backers for comprehensive practices. Maya's story becomes significant of the more extensive subject of local area commitment, accentuating the job of people with chemical imbalance as dynamic supporters of the social texture. Wins in this domain include the production of tactile cordial local area spaces, the advancement of comprehensive occasions, and the acknowledgment of the important commitments people with mental imbalance make to the networks in which they live.

Family Backing and Joint effort: A Significant Point of support

All through the moves and wins of the change to adulthood for people with mental imbalance, the job of family backing and joint effort arises as a pivotal support point. Families assume an instrumental part in offering profound help, upholding for their friends and family, and teaming up with teachers, managers, and networks to establish conditions that cultivate consideration.

Consider the tale of Olivia, a young lady with chemical imbalance, whose family effectively teams up with teachers to guarantee her outcome in advanced education. Olivia's story mirrors the more extensive topic of family support, featuring the significance of open correspondence, understanding, and dynamic joint effort among families and different partners. Wins in this domain include the formation of encouraging groups of people, family schooling drives, and cooperative endeavors that perceive and value the special qualities and necessities of people with mental imbalance.

All in all, the difficulties and valuable open doors for people with chemical imbalance entering adulthood structure a unique story that envelops schooling, work, social elements, free living, emotional well-being, legitimate backing, monetary autonomy, post-optional training, local area commitment, and family coordinated effort. A story requires an aggregate obligation to cultivating comprehensive conditions, destroying foundational hindrances, and perceiving the innate worth and potential inside the chemical imbalance local area. By embracing neurodiversity, focusing on individual qualities, and cultivating a general public that obliges different requirements, we can make a more comprehensive and evenhanded reality where people with mental imbalance can explore the progress to adulthood with flexibility, nobility, and the chance to contribute definitively to the embroidery of human encounters.

7.2 Employment, higher education, and independent living.

Work, Advanced education, and Free Living: A Comprehensive Investigation of Adulthood

The progress from youthfulness to adulthood is an extraordinary excursion set apart by critical achievements, and key to this excursion are the interwoven parts of business, advanced education, and free living. This story dives into the multi-layered scene of these essential parts, investigating the difficulties, wins, and the advancing idea of the grown-up experience.

Business: Exploring Profession Ways and Comprehensive Work areas

The domain of work remains as a foundation of grown-up life, enveloping the method for monetary food as well as a wellspring of character, reason, and social joining. For people changing into adulthood, the scene of work can be both promising and testing. The story unfurls as they explore vocation ways, defy cultural assumptions, and take a stab at significant work encounters.

Challenges inside the work domain for some people include getting through cultural predispositions and generalizations. This is particularly valid for those with neurodivergent conditions, like chemical imbalance. The account investigates the encounters of people like Alex, who confronted beginning obstacles because of misguided judgments about their capacities. Wins inside this domain include getting work as well as supporting for comprehensive work environments, where different abilities are perceived and esteemed.

Comprehensive business rehearses become a significant topic in the story, with an emphasis on cultivating neurodiversity mindfulness among managers. Drives that advance sensible facilities, tactile amicable workplaces, and customized help components become critical victories in guaranteeing that people with changing capacities can contribute seriously to the labor force.

Advanced education: Chasing after Information and Incorporation

The quest for advanced education is an extraordinary excursion that opens ways to scholarly development, extended viewpoints, and different open doors. Be that as it may, for people changing to adulthood, getting to advanced education can be loaded with difficulties connected with scholastic facilities, social mix, and a more extensive acknowledgment of neurodiversity inside instructive foundations.

The story unfurls as people like Maya explore the intricacies of advanced education. Difficulties might emerge in getting to suitable facilities, like tangible agreeable spaces and steady learning conditions. Wins inside this domain include scholarly accomplishment as well as the advancement of neurodiversity inside instructive settings, cultivating a comprehensive culture that perceives and obliges different learning styles.

Comprehensive advanced education rehearses become a urgent part of the story, underlining the significance of open assets, peer support, and the development of a learning climate that celebrates contrasts. The victories inside this domain include getting degrees as well as adding to the making of a comprehensive instructive scene that supports the capability of each and every understudy.

Free Living: Encouraging Independence and Comprehensive People group

The idea of free living is unpredictably attached to the more extensive account of adulthood, typifying the capacity to deal with one's undertakings, explore the intricacies of day to day existence, and add to the local area. For people changing to adulthood, particularly those with different capacities, free living addresses both an individual goal and a cultural test.

Challenges inside the domain of autonomous living might include dominating fundamental abilities, exploring public spaces, and guaranteeing openness. The story unfurls as people like James set out on an excursion to master fundamental abilities, from cooking to utilizing public transportation. Wins inside this domain include accomplishing individual independence as well as adding to the production of comprehensive networks that oblige different necessities.

Comprehensive living practices become a critical subject in the story, under-scoring the significance of upheld living plans, local area drives, and open public spaces. The victories inside this domain include individual freedom as well as adding to cultural movements that perceive and value the extraordinary qualities and commitments of people with different capacities.

Interconnection and All encompassing Methodologies

As the story of business, advanced education, and autonomous living unfurls, the interconnection of these parts becomes evident. People with different capacities explore a scene where these perspectives entwine, impacting each other in signifi-cant ways. Difficulties and wins in a single domain frequently have resonations in others, stressing the requirement for all encompassing methodologies that address the interconnected idea of adulthood.

Think about the tale of Sarah, a young lady with mental imbalance, who succeeded in her advanced education pursuits as well as confronted moves in the work environment because of misguided judgments about her capacities. Sarah's story mirrors the interconnection of business and advanced education, featuring the requirement for incorporated emotionally supportive networks that address the assorted parts of grown-up life.

All encompassing methodologies include perceiving the interconnectedness of business, advanced education, and autonomous living, and encouraging drives that think about the entire person. This incorporates far reaching emotionally support-ive networks that stretch out from instructive organizations to the work environ-ment and local area living spaces. The victories inside this account include the making of consistent advances, where people can move from instructive settings to profitable business and free residing with satisfactory help at each step.

Psychological wellness and Prosperity in Adulthood

Inside the account of business, advanced education, and autonomous living, emotional wellness and prosperity arise as essential contemplations. The diffi-culties looked by people progressing to adulthood might influence their close to home scene, requiring a nuanced comprehension of the crossing points between emotional wellness and the different parts of grown-up life.

Challenges inside the psychological wellness domain might include overseeing uneasiness, exploring tangible awarenesses, and adjusting to evolving conditions. The account unfurls as people, families, and encouraging groups of people effectively take part in cultivating strength and prosperity. Wins inside this domain include the prioritization of psychological wellness conversations, self-promotion, and the production of strong conditions that oblige the remarkable feelings of people changing to adulthood.

Consider the tale of David, a youthful grown-up with chemical imbalance, who effectively looks for help during testing times and turns into a backer for emotional wellness mindfulness. David's story mirrors the more extensive subject of emotional wellness contemplations in adulthood, underlining the significance of open psychological well-being administrations, tangible cordial spaces, and an all encompassing way to deal with prosperity.

Advanced Spaces and Network in Grown-up Life

The contemporary account of adulthood is unpredictably woven with the job of advanced spaces, innovation, and availability. In the domains of work, advanced education, and free living, people explore a scene molded by computerized communications, virtual entertainment, and online stages. The difficulties and wins inside this domain add to the advancing idea of grown-up encounters.

Challenges inside the advanced scene might include dealing with the arranged idea of online characters, managing social examination, and tending to potential cyberbullying. The story unfurls as people like Mia effectively deal with their computerized presence to encourage a solid mental self view and credible associations. Wins inside this domain include computerized education, the development of positive internet based networks, and the acknowledgment of the expected effect of advanced spaces on mental and profound prosperity.

Consider the tale of Mia as symbolic of the more extensive subject of utilizing computerized spaces for positive self-articulation while effectively tending to the difficulties presented by the web-based world. Comprehensive practices inside advanced spaces include advancing computerized education, making safe web-based networks, and perceiving the job of innovation in improving the general grown-up experience.

Social and Cultural Assumptions in Adulthood

The account of adulthood is likewise molded by social and cultural assumptions that people should explore. Social foundations, orientation personality, and financial variables impact the focal point through which people view themselves and are seen by society. The difficulties and wins inside this domain add to the intricacy of the grown-up experience.

Challenges inside the social and cultural scene might include exploring assumptions connected with profession decisions, family designs, and individual desires. The story unfurls as people like Raj face social assumptions about unambiguous vocation ways. Wins inside this domain include the festival of different personalities, the dismissal of restricting generalizations, and the cultivating of comprehensive conditions that honor individual decisions.

Consider the narrative of Raj as meaningful of the more extensive difficulties looked by people exploring the convergence of social practices and individual goals. Comprehensive practices inside social and cultural settings include advancing variety, testing generalizations, and establishing conditions that permit people to communicate their personalities genuinely.

Determination: Winding around a Comprehensive Embroidery of Adulthood

The story of business, advanced education, and free living weaves a comprehensive embroidery of adulthood, rich with difficulties, wins, and the interconnected idea of individual encounters. As people progress into this extraordinary phase of life, they explore scenes formed by cultural assumptions, advanced spaces, social subtleties, and the crossing points of work, schooling, and free living.

Comprehensive methodologies include perceiving the assorted qualities and requirements of people changing to adulthood, cultivating comprehensive practices that stretch out across instructive foundations, working environments, and living spaces.

The victories inside this story are not separated; they add to the production of a general public that values neurodiversity, embraces individual contrasts, and gives significant open doors to each grown-up, no matter what their extraordinary capacities.

The excursion of adulthood is a unique cycle, and as the story unfurls, obviously no single perspective works in seclusion. Work, advanced education, and free living are interconnected strings that, when woven along with compassion, understanding, and inclusivity, structure an embroidery that commends the different and exceptional encounters of people changing into adulthood. By embracing the intricacy of this story, society can add to establishing a climate where each individual can flourish, understanding their maximum capacity and contributing seriously to the assorted woven artwork of human encounters.

7.3 Strategies for supporting a successful transition.

Techniques for Supporting an Effective Change to Adulthood: Sustaining Development and Freedom

The progress from pre-adulthood to adulthood is a basic crossroads in a singular's life, set apart by huge changes and recently discovered liabilities. Supporting a fruitful change requires a smart and exhaustive methodology that thinks about the different necessities and qualities of every person. This story investigates procedures pointed toward encouraging an effective change to adulthood, including regions like schooling, business, free living, and generally prosperity.

1. **Individual Focused Arranging: Fitting Help to Individual Necessities**

   At the core of effective progress arranging is the reception of individual focused approaches that focus on the interesting necessities, inclinations, and desires of every person. Individual focused arranging includes coordinated effort between the individual, their family, teachers, and encouraging groups of people to make a tweaked guide for the progress to adulthood. This procedure guarantees that mediations and support systems line up with the singular's objectives, advancing a feeling of organization and self-assurance.

   Consider the narrative of Maya, a young lady with chemical imbalance, whose change plan was made through individual focused arranging. This approach permitted Maya to verbalize her inclinations and objectives, molding her instructive excursion and preparing for significant work. Individual focused arranging wins in perceiving and praising the singularity of every individual, cultivating a feeling of responsibility in their progress cycle.

2. **Early Mediation and Backing: Building Starting points for Progress**

   Early mediation assumes a significant part in supporting an effective progress, especially for people with different capacities. Recognizing qualities and difficulties almost immediately takes into consideration designated intercessions and backing administrations. Support, both self-backing and outside promotion, is vital to guaranteeing that people get the assets and facilities required for a smooth progress.

   Think about the story of David, who, with early mediation and solid promotion, defeated difficulties related with a learning inability. Early ID and customized help administrations tended to David's scholarly necessities as well as engaged him to advocate for himself as he progressed into advanced education and business. Early mediation and backing wins in laying the basis for progress, underscoring the significance of proactive measures to help people as they explore the intricacies of adulthood.

3. **Comprehensive Instruction Works on: Supporting Long lasting Learning**

   Comprehensive instruction rehearses structure a foundation for an effective change, encouraging a climate where people with different capacities can learn and flourish close by their friends. Comprehensive schooling includes adjusting educational plans, giving fundamental facilities, and making a strong environment that values neurodiversity. This methodology upgrades scholastic results as well as sustains interactive abilities and a feeling of having a place.

   Consider the account of Chris, whose positive involvement with a comprehensive instructive setting established the groundwork for his effective change into adulthood. Comprehensive training rehearses win in stalling obstructions, cultivating positive friend connections, and getting ready people for the more extensive cultural scene. The progress of comprehensive training stretches out past scholarly accomplishments to the development of abilities fundamental for an effective change.

4. **Professional Preparation and Ability Advancement: Overcoming any issues to Work**

Getting ready people for the labor force includes designated professional preparation and ability advancement programs. These drives overcome any barrier among instruction and work by giving commonsense abilities and involved encounters. Professional preparation not just outfits people with the abilities expected for explicit positions yet additionally ingrains certainty and a feeling of direction.

Consider the story of Alex, who took part in a professional preparation program zeroed in on innovation abilities. This program upgraded Alex's employability as well as filled in as a demonstration of the viability of designated expertise improvement drives. Professional preparation and expertise advancement win in engaging people to enter the labor force with certainty, overcoming any barrier among training and significant business.

5. **Progress Administrations and Far reaching Arranging: Tending to All encompassing Requirements**

Thorough progress administrations include a scope of supports intended to address the all encompassing necessities of people as they explore the change to adulthood. This incorporates instructive preparation, profession directing, free living abilities preparing, and emotional wellness support. An organized and far reaching approach guarantees that people get the essential assets and direction across different spaces of their lives.

Consider the tale of Emma, who profited from an exhaustive progress plan that included scholarly help, vocation direction, and help with creating free living abilities. Far reaching arranging wins in recognizing the multi-layered nature of the change cycle, offering customized arrangements that address individual qualities and difficulties. This approach guarantees a smoother progress by giving a guide that considers instructive, professional, and individual objectives.

6. **Mentorship and Friend Backing: Encouraging Social Associations**

The job of mentorship and companion support couldn't possibly be more significant in supporting a fruitful progress. Laying out associations with tutors who have encountered comparative advances gives important experiences and direction. Peer support, whether through help gatherings or casual organizations, cultivates a feeling of local area and shared encounters, decreasing sensations of segregation.

Consider the story of Olivia, who found mentorship and companion support instrumental in exploring the difficulties of advanced education. Mentorship and friend support win in giving people good examples, a feeling of having a place, and commonsense guidance on overseeing different parts of adulthood. These associations add to the improvement of interactive abilities, self-assurance, and an emotionally supportive network that is important during the progress.

7. **Innovation and Assistive Devices: Upgrading Autonomy**

In the computerized age, innovation and assistive devices assume a urgent part in upgrading freedom for people with different capacities. These devices can support correspondence, using time productively, association, and getting to data. Integrating innovation into progress plans enables people to conquer explicit difficulties and partake all the more completely in training, work, and day to day existence.

Consider the narrative of James, who used assistive innovation to improve his autonomous living abilities. The joining of innovation wins in separating obstructions and giving people devices that take special care of their exceptional necessities. From specialized gadgets to applications that help association, innovation turns into a strong partner in advancing freedom during the progress to adulthood.

8. **Local area Commitment and Incorporation: Building Social Capital**

Local area commitment and incorporation systems center around coordinating people into local area life, encouraging a feeling of having a place, and building social capital. Partaking in local area exercises, chipping in, and drawing in with neighborhood associations add to a more extensive comprehension of cultural assumptions and give potential open doors to expertise improvement.

Consider the story of Maya, who effectively participates in local area occasions and supporters for comprehensive practices. Local area commitment wins in making associations, growing informal communities, and imparting a feeling of obligation and commitment. These encounters add to the improvement of interactive abilities, expand points of view, and build up the possibility that people with assorted capacities have significant commitments to make to their networks.

9. **Monetary Proficiency Training: Engaging Autonomy**

Monetary proficiency training is a basic part of supporting a fruitful change to adulthood. Furnishing people with the information and abilities to oversee funds, spending plan really, and settle on informed choices enables them to autonomously explore the financial scene. Monetary proficiency schooling guarantees that people can go with sound monetary decisions and plan for their future.

Consider the account of Ryan, who effectively taught himself on monetary education and came to informed conclusions about saving and financial planning. Monetary proficiency training wins in outfitting people with the apparatuses to accomplish monetary autonomy, pursue vital decisions, and explore the financial real factors of adulthood with certainty.

10. Continuum of Help Administrations: Past Progress Period

Perceiving that the progress to adulthood is definitely not a limited cycle yet a consistent excursion highlights the significance of laying out a continuum of help administrations. These administrations stretch out past the proper progress period, offering continuous help as people explore the intricacies of grown-up life. A consistent continuum of help administrations guarantees that people can get to help while required, advancing supported freedom and development.

Consider the story of Elena, who effectively looks for open doors for ceaseless learning and self-improvement. A continuum of help administrations wins in recognizing that the excursion of progressing to adulthood is continuous, with developing requirements and difficulties. By offering progressing help, people can explore different life stages with strength, versatility, and a guarantee to persistent improvement.

Decision: A Cooperative and Comprehensive Methodology

All in all, supporting an effective change to adulthood includes a cooperative and comprehensive methodology that tends to the novel requirements and qualities of every person. Individual focused arranging, early mediation, comprehensive schooling rehearses, professional preparation, far reaching arranging, mentorship, innovation mix, local area commitment, monetary proficiency instruction, and a continuum of help benefits on the whole add to an all encompassing structure.

The victories inside every system feature the groundbreaking effect of custom fitted help components that perceive the variety of encounters during the progress to adulthood. By encouraging a cooperative and comprehensive climate, society can add to the strengthening of people, advancing their development, freedom, and significant support in the embroidery of grown-up life. The progress of these methodologies lies in their singular benefits as well as in their aggregate capacity to make a steady environment that sustains the capability of each and every individual changing into adulthood.

Chapter 8

Workplace Inclusion
Unleashing Potential

Working environment Consideration: Releasing Likely in the Cutting edge Labor force

In the powerful scene of the cutting edge labor force, the idea of work environment consideration has developed past being a simple popular expression — it has turned into a major driver of progress, development, and representative prosperity. This story investigates the multi-layered components of work environment consideration, digging into its importance, difficulties, and wins as associations endeavor to open the maximum capacity of a different and skilled labor force.

Figuring out Working environment Consideration: Past Variety Measurements

Working environment incorporation reaches out past the mathematical portrayal of variety; it typifies a culture and climate where people from different foundations, encounters, and points of view feel esteemed, heard, and enabled. It includes encouraging a feeling of having a place, destroying foundational obstructions, and effectively advancing value inside the association.

The victory of working environment consideration lies in its capacity to move past simple variety measurements to make a climate that perceives and celebrates individual contrasts. This approach guarantees that the association benefits from a rich embroidery of points of view, thoughts, and gifts, at last prompting upgraded innovativeness, critical thinking, and by and large execution.

Challenges in Accomplishing Genuine Consideration: Separating Hindrances

While the significance of working environment incorporation is broadly recognized, accomplishing it stays a perplexing test. Obstructions might incorporate oblivious inclinations, fundamental imbalances, and authoritative designs that accidentally thwart the full interest of different people. Addressing these difficulties requires a deliberate work to distinguish and destroy imbued rehearses that propagate prohibition.

Consider the narrative of Sarah, an expert who confronted unpretentious predispositions in her working environment, frustrating her expert development. Sarah's story mirrors the more extensive difficulties people experience, underlining the requirement for associations to proactively distinguish and take out boundaries to genuine consideration. The victories in separating these hindrances include developing mindfulness, giving coaching in racial awareness, and cultivating a culture of responsibility that effectively challenges exclusionary rehearses.

Comprehensive Initiative: Establishing the Vibe from the Top

One of the urgent victories in accomplishing work environment consideration lies in the responsibility of authority to support variety and consideration as basic beliefs. Comprehensive administration includes establishing the vibe from the top, where pioneers effectively develop a climate that qualities and use the extraordinary commitments of each and every person. Initiative responsibility isn't just an emblematic signal yet an impetus for significant change inside the association.

Consider the story of Alex, who encountered the groundbreaking effect of comprehensive authority when the President effectively supported variety drives. Comprehensive initiative victories by making a hierarchical culture that pervades all levels, cultivating a feeling of having a place and empowering representatives to carry their legitimate selves to work. At the point when pioneers focus on and model comprehensive ways of behaving, it makes way for the whole association to go with the same pattern.

Worker Asset Gatherings and Proclivity Organizations: Building Steady People group

Worker asset gatherings (ERGs) and proclivity networks are instrumental in making steady networks inside the working environment. These gatherings give a space to people with shared qualities, encounters, or foundations to interface, share bits of knowledge, and promoter for inclusivity. ERGs win by enhancing the voices of underrepresented gatherings and cultivating a feeling of local area that rises above proficient limits.

Consider the narrative of Emma, who found help and mentorship through a partiality network for ladies in her industry. The victories of ERGs lie in their capacity to make a feeling of local area, offer mentorship potential open doors, and supporter for strategies that advance inclusivity. At the point when people find support inside these gatherings, it adds to their general work fulfillment, commitment, and feeling of strengthening.

Adaptable Work Courses of action: Obliging Different Requirements

The cutting edge labor force flourishes with adaptability, and associations embracing comprehensive practices perceive the significance of obliging assorted needs. Adaptable work game plans, including remote work choices, adaptable hours, and elective work structures, win by permitting people to offset proficient obligations with individual responsibilities.

Think about the story of James, who, because of a handicap, benefitted enormously from an adaptable work plan that permitted him to deal with his work such that fit his necessities. The victories of adaptable work game plans lie in their capacity to upgrade balance between serious and fun activities, oblige different capacities, and draw in a more extensive pool of ability that might have in any case been rejected because of unbending work structures.

Preparing and Instruction Drives: Cultivating Comprehensive Mentalities

Instructive drives and preparing programs are fundamental parts of winning over the difficulties of work environment incorporation. Associations that put resources into racial awareness coaching, social capability projects, and mindfulness crusades make a labor force that is better prepared to comprehend, appreciate, and explore the intricacies of a different work environment.

Consider the narrative of David, who went through racial awareness schooling that reshaped his viewpoint and conduct towards associates from various foundations. The victories of preparing drives lie in their capacity to develop comprehensive mentalities, break down generalizations, and encourage a culture of regard and understanding. These projects add to establishing a more comprehensive workplace where people feel seen, heard, and regarded.

Availability and Facilities: Evening the odds

Comprehensive work environments focus on availability and facilities to guarantee that people with different capacities can completely take part in all parts of expert life. From actual availability in office spaces to giving assistive advancements, associations win in making everything fair when they effectively put resources into establishing a climate that obliges the requirements, all things considered.

Consider the story of Mia, who encountered the extraordinary effect of work environment facilities that permitted her to perform at her best. The victories in openness and facilities include meeting lawful prerequisites as well as effectively looking for ways of establishing a comprehensive climate where everybody, paying little heed to capacity, can contribute definitively.

Straightforward Strategies and Responsibility Measures: Building Trust

Associations that hero work environment consideration have straightforward strategies set up that address variety, value, and incorporation. These strategies, combined with responsibility measures, win by cultivating a feeling of trust among workers. At the point when people see that the association is focused on considering itself responsible for establishing a comprehensive climate, it adds to a culture of receptiveness and decency.

Consider the account of Raj, who valued the straightforward approaches that tended to variety and incorporation in his work environment. The victories in straightforward strategies and responsibility measures include making a culture where people feel certain that their interests will be tended to and that the association is effectively pursuing making an impartial work environment.

Estimating and Observing Achievement: Perceiving Progress

Win in work environment consideration includes carrying out drives as well as estimating and commending achievement. Associations that consistently evaluate their variety and consideration endeavors, celebrate accomplishments, and recognize regions for development exhibit a guarantee to ceaseless development and improvement in encouraging a comprehensive work environment.

Consider the account of Maya, who saw the positive effect of her association's yearly variety and incorporation report, featuring accomplishments and illustrating future objectives. The victories in estimating and praising achievement lie in making a culture of responsibility, where representatives feel esteemed, and the association effectively pursues turning out to be more comprehensive over the long run.

Worldwide Viewpoints and Culturally diverse Capability: Exploring a Worldwide Labor force

In an undeniably interconnected world, associations should explore the subtleties of a worldwide labor force. Win in working environment consideration includes embracing worldwide points of view, advancing multifaceted skill, and perceiving the extravagance that variety brings to the association's worldwide character.

Consider the narrative of Ryan, who flourished in a working environment that effectively advanced multifaceted skill and esteemed the commitments of representatives from different social foundations. The victories in worldwide viewpoints and multifaceted skill include making a work environment where people from various regions of the planet feel appreciated, comprehended, and appreciated for their special viewpoints.

Developing a Culture of Consideration

All in all, work environment consideration wins when associations develop a culture that values variety, value, and consideration as fundamental parts of their character. The diverse systems investigated, from comprehensive authority to adaptable work game plans, straightforwardness in arrangements, and worldwide points of view, on the whole add to establishing a climate where people can release their maximum capacity.

The victories in working environment consideration reach out past simple hierarchical achievement; they add to the more extensive cultural account of destroying fundamental obstructions and encouraging conditions where everybody, paying little mind to foundation or personality, can flourish. As associations effectively seek after and celebrate working environment consideration, they become drivers of financial accomplishment as well as guides of progress and value in a world that undeniably esteems the strength tracked down in variety.

8.1 The role of employers in fostering a neurodiverse workforce.

The Job of Managers in Cultivating a Neurodiverse Labor force: Supporting Ability and Driving Development

In the developing scene of the cutting edge working environment, there is a developing acknowledgment of the significance of neurodiversity — an idea that underlines the normal variety in neurological capacities among people. Bosses assume a significant part in cultivating a neurodiverse labor force, contributing not exclusively to the prosperity of representatives yet in addition to the development and progress of the association. This account investigates the multi-layered job of bosses in embracing neurodiversity, tending to difficulties, and prevailing in establishing comprehensive and enabling workplaces.

Grasping Neurodiversity: Past Ordinary Points of view

Neurodiversity challenges the traditional comprehension of neurological contrasts, featuring the variety of cerebrum capability and cognizance. It envelops conditions like chemical imbalance, ADHD, dyslexia, and other neurological varieties. Perceiving and embracing neurodiversity implies moving past a shortage based point of view to one that values the interesting qualities and viewpoints that neurodivergent people offer of real value.

The victory of understanding neurodiversity lies in moving the story from zeroing in exclusively on difficulties to perceiving and utilizing the extraordinary gifts and capacities that neurodivergent people have. Businesses who comprehend the worth of neurodiversity encourage a climate where various abilities and creative reasoning flourish, adding to the general outcome of the association.

Making Comprehensive Employing Works on: Taking advantage of Different Ability

One of the significant jobs managers play in cultivating a neurodiverse labor force is through the making of comprehensive employing rehearses. Conventional enlistment cycles may unintentionally prohibit neurodivergent people because of inclinations or an absence of mindfulness. Win in this domain includes executing methodologies that effectively look for and embrace neurodiverse ability.

Consider the tale of Chris, who battled to find work until he experienced an organization with comprehensive recruiting rehearses. The victory of comprehensive recruiting lies in perceiving the qualities and expected commitments of neurodivergent people. Managers who effectively look to enhance their ability pool benefit from a scope of points of view and abilities that can drive development and critical thinking inside the association.

Fitting the Workplace: Facilities and Openness

Making a neurodiverse labor force expects managers to tailor the workplace to oblige the different necessities of their representatives. This includes giving sensible facilities, guaranteeing physical and tactile availability, and encouraging an air where neurodivergent people feel good and upheld.

The victory of fitting the workplace lies in the capacity to make a comprehensive space where neurodivergent representatives can perform at their best. Managers who put resources into making their working environments open send a reasonable message that they esteem the commitments, everything being equal, paying little mind to neurological contrasts. This approach not just improves the prosperity of neurodivergent people yet in addition adds to a more useful and agreeable workplace.

Advancing Neurodiversity Mindfulness: Preparing and Instruction Drives

Businesses assume a vital part in advancing neurodiversity mindfulness among their labor force. Preparing and training drives that cultivate a comprehension of neurodivergent conditions, diminish shame, and furnish pragmatic bits of knowledge into working with neurodivergent partners add to a more comprehensive work environment culture.

The victory of neurodiversity mindfulness lies in the making of a steady and compassionate workplace. Businesses who focus on continuous training on neurodiversity guarantee that their labor force is prepared to associate, team up, and discuss successfully with partners who have assorted neurological profiles. By encouraging a culture of understanding, businesses add to a work environment where everybody feels esteemed and regarded.

Mentorship and Companion Backing Projects: Supporting Proficient Development

Bosses can additionally advocate neurodiversity by executing mentorship and friend support programs. These drives furnish neurodivergent workers with direction, backing, and valuable open doors for proficient turn of events. The victory of mentorship and companion support lies in the strengthening of neurodivergent people to effectively explore their vocations.

Consider the story of Olivia, who benefited incredibly from a mentorship program that assisted her with exploring the intricacies of the work environment. Businesses who focus on mentorship and companion support add to the individual and expert development of neurodivergent representatives. These projects make a feeling of local area, cultivate expertise improvement, and give significant organizations that can add to long haul profession achievement.

Adaptable Work Courses of action: Recognizing Assorted Work Styles

Recognizing and obliging different work styles is a critical part of encouraging a neurodiverse labor force. Bosses who offer adaptable work plans, for example, remote work choices or versatile timetables, win in perceiving that neurodivergent people might flourish in conditions that take care of their novel requirements.

The victory of adaptable work plans lies in establishing a workplace where neurodivergent representatives can accomplish their best outcomes. Bosses who embrace adaptability oblige different correspondence styles, tactile requirements, and work inclinations, adding to expanded work fulfillment and generally speaking prosperity among neurodivergent people.

Backing and Allyship: Enabling Neurodivergent Representatives

Bosses assume a crucial part in supporting for neurodiversity and cultivating allyship inside the work environment. This includes making a culture where partners effectively backing and promoter for neurodivergent people, adding to a more comprehensive and compassionate climate.

Consider the narrative of David, who tracked down strengthening through the support of his partners. The victory of promotion and allyship lies in the making of a working environment where neurodivergent people are acknowledged as well as effectively upheld. Bosses who encourage allyship add to a culture of consideration, where neurodivergent workers feel engaged to contribute their special viewpoints and gifts.

Assessing and Changing Approaches: Consistent Improvement

Businesses focused on encouraging a neurodiverse labor force participate in the persistent assessment and change of their strategies. This incorporates inspecting enrollment rehearses, convenience strategies, and generally speaking work environment culture to recognize regions for development and carry out fundamental changes.

The victory of assessing and changing approaches lies in the obligation to persistent improvement. Businesses who routinely survey their strategies for neurodiversity inclusivity show a commitment to making a developing and versatile work environment. This approach guarantees that the association stays receptive to the requirements of neurodivergent representatives and reliably pursues encouraging a more comprehensive climate.

Making Neurodiversity Representative Asset Gatherings (ERGs): Building People group

Laying out Neurodiversity Representative Asset Gatherings (ERGs) can be a strong technique for managers hoping to encourage a neurodiverse labor force. These gatherings give a stage to workers to share encounters, offer common help, and team up on drives that advance neurodiversity inside the association.

The victory of Neurodiversity ERGs lies in their capacity to make a feeling of local area and brotherhood among neurodivergent workers. Managers who work with the development of these gatherings add to the general prosperity of neurodivergent people, while likewise saddling the aggregate experiences of these gatherings to illuminate authoritative practices and approaches.

Estimating Accomplishment Through Neurodiversity Measurements: Responsibility

Managers can win in encouraging a neurodiverse labor force by integrating neurodiversity measurements into their assessment systems. Estimating achievement includes following the portrayal, maintenance, and progression of neurodivergent representatives, guaranteeing responsibility and straightforwardness in the association's obligation to variety and consideration.

Consider the account of Maya, who noticed positive changes in her work environment after the execution of neurodiversity measurements. The victory of estimating accomplishment through neurodiversity measurements lies in considering the association responsible for its objectives and responsibilities. Businesses who consistently survey and report on neurodiversity measurements add to a culture of straightforwardness and exhibit a certifiable obligation to encouraging a comprehensive working environment.

Extraordinary Effect of Neurodiversity in the Work environment

All in all, the job of bosses in encouraging a neurodiverse labor force is extraordinary, impacting the singular encounters of neurodivergent workers as well as the general achievement and development of the association. The victories investigated, from comprehensive recruiting practices to adaptable work plans, mentorship projects, and neurodiversity ERGs, on the whole add to making working environments where variety is praised, and each individual is enabled to release their maximum capacity.

As bosses progressively perceive the worth of neurodiversity, they become pioneers in forming a future where work environments blossom with the strength of different personalities and points of view. The excursion towards a neurodiverse labor force is progressing, set apart by consistent learning, transformation, and a promise to encouraging conditions where each person, paying little mind to neurological contrasts, can prosper and contribute definitively to the aggregate outcome of the association.

8.2 Success stories of companies embracing inclusive hiring practices.

Examples of overcoming adversity of Organizations Embracing Comprehensive Recruiting Works on: Spearheading Variety and Flourishing in the Advanced Work environment

In the contemporary scene of the business world, organizations are progressively perceiving the extraordinary force of comprehensive employing rehearses.

This account investigates examples of overcoming adversity of organizations that have embraced variety and incorporation, exhibiting how comprehensive recruiting rehearses enhance the labor force as well as add to development, worker fulfillment, and by and large achievement.

Salesforce: A Pioneer in Uniformity

Salesforce, a worldwide forerunner in client relationship the executives (CRM) programming, has set up a good foundation for itself as a pioneer in the domain of work environment correspondence and consideration. The organization's obligation to cultivating a different labor force is exemplified through essential drives and strategies effectively advance inclusivity.

One of Salesforce's vital accomplishments is accomplishing orientation pay fairness, as the organization deliberately investigated and changed pay rates to guarantee impartial pay for representatives regardless of orientation. Furthermore, Salesforce has taken huge steps in expanding its initiative group, with an emphasis on selecting ladies to chief positions. The progress of Salesforce lies in its obligation to inclusivity as well as in its proactive way to deal with tending to abberations and supporting equity all through the association.

Microsoft: A Guarantee to Neurodiversity

Microsoft, an innovation monster, has exhibited a significant obligation to neurodiversity through its Chemical imbalance Employing Project. Perceiving the novel gifts and abilities that neurodivergent people bring to the innovation area, Microsoft effectively tries to utilize people on the chemical imbalance range. The organization's program includes an intensive enrollment process that underlines a singular's capacities as opposed to zeroing in exclusively on customary recruiting measures.

Microsoft's outcome in embracing neurodiversity is obvious in the assorted points of view and imaginative arrangements that neurodivergent representatives add to the organization's ventures. By establishing a strong and understanding workplace, Microsoft has not just given significant business potential open doors to neurodivergent people however has likewise improved its labor force with a more extensive scope of gifts and viewpoints.

Accenture: Focusing on Incorporation Across the Globe

Accenture, a worldwide expert administrations organization, has situated itself as a signal of comprehensive employing rehearses across the globe. The organization's obligation to variety is reflected in its drives to make a labor force that reflects the variety of the networks it serves. Accenture has carried out designated endeavors to build the portrayal of underrepresented gatherings, including ladies, ethnic minorities, and people with inabilities.

One of Accenture's fruitful methodologies is its obligation to straightforwardness, consistently distributing variety measurements and setting clear focuses for development. By cultivating a culture of responsibility and persistent improvement, Accenture has drawn in different ability as well as established a climate where people from all foundations feel esteemed and upheld in their expert development.

IBM: Developing with Mental Capacities

IBM, a global innovation and counseling organization, has embraced comprehensive recruiting rehearses with a specific spotlight on people with mental capacities. Through its "P-TECH" (Pathways in Innovation Early School Secondary School) program, IBM has attempted to overcome any barrier among training and work for neurodivergent people. The program furnishes understudies with the abilities and backing required for outcome in the innovation business.

IBM's progress in comprehensive recruiting is exemplified by the different ability pool that adds to the organization's advancement and critical thinking capacities. By effectively looking for neurodivergent people and making pathways for their expert turn of events, IBM has enhanced its labor force as well as started a trend for different organizations to saddle the special qualities of people with mental capacities.

JPMorgan Pursue: A Promise to Variety and Incorporation

JPMorgan Pursue, a main worldwide monetary administrations firm, has taken critical steps in encouraging variety and consideration inside its labor force. The organization's obligation to making a fair working environment is exhibited through thorough variety and consideration drives include enrollment, progression, and authority advancement.

One of JPMorgan Pursue's triumphs lies in its obligation to tending to racial and orientation abberations in the monetary business. The organization has executed designated projects to increment portrayal at all levels and has effectively taken part in local area drives to advance monetary consideration. JPMorgan Pursue's obligation to variety and consideration isn't just clear in its labor force sythesis yet additionally in its commitment to making positive social effect past its authoritative limits.

SAP: Focusing on Capacities Over Incapacities

SAP, a worldwide programming organization, has turned into a pioneer in focusing on capacities over handicaps through its Chemical imbalance working project. Perceiving the undiscovered possibility of people on the chemical imbalance range, SAP has effectively enrolled and incorporated neurodivergent workers into different jobs inside the organization.

The progress of SAP's comprehensive recruiting rehearses is clear in the positive results for both the organization and its neurodivergent workers. Through mentorship programs, work environment facilities, and a pledge to encouraging a comprehensive culture, SAP has established a climate where neurodivergent people can flourish. By zeroing in on capacities, SAP has expanded variety as well as reclassified biases about the commitments of people with chemical imbalance in the corporate world.

Walmart: A Guarantee to Variety in Retail

Walmart, a retail monster, has exhibited a promise to variety and incorporation across its huge organization of stores. The organization has carried out comprehensive employing rehearses that focus on equivalent open doors for all people, regardless of foundation or personality. Walmart's progress in cultivating variety is remarkable in an industry where portrayal can frequently be a test.

Walmart's obligation to comprehensive recruiting stretches out to programs that help the work of military veterans, people with incapacities, and people reappearing the labor force. The organization has expanded portrayal as well as established a workplace where representatives from different foundations feel esteemed and upheld in their expert processes.

Google: Utilizing Variety for Advancement

Google, a worldwide innovation organization, has for quite some time been perceived for its obligation to cultivating a different and comprehensive labor force. Google's progress in comprehensive recruiting rehearses is highlighted by its essential drives to increment portrayal across different elements of variety, including orientation, race, and nationality.

One of Google's victories is its attention on making a comprehensive culture that use variety for development. The organization effectively upholds representative asset gatherings, mentorship projects, and drives that enable underrepresented gatherings. Google's obligation to variety upgrades its ability pool as well as adds to a culture of development, where various viewpoints drive imaginative critical thinking and mechanical progressions.

Procter and Bet: Variety as a Business Basic

Procter and Bet (P&G), a worldwide customer products partnership, has embraced variety as a business basic, perceiving that a different labor force is fundamental for understanding and addressing the requirements of a different shopper base. P&G's outcome in comprehensive employing is apparent in its obligation to approach portrayal and progression amazing open doors for people from all foundations.

P&G's victory lies in its emphasis on variety as an upper hand as opposed to only an ethical goal. The organization effectively looks for different points of view to illuminate item advancement, advertising procedures, and business choices. By focusing on variety in its labor force, P&G has not just made a working environment where representatives feel esteemed however has likewise situated itself for supported progress in a universally serious market.

Bank of America: Variety and Incorporation as Fundamental beliefs

Bank of America, a main monetary establishment, has implanted variety and incorporation as guiding principle inside its hierarchical culture. The organization's outcome in cultivating variety is shown through exhaustive methodology tends to enlistment as well as authority improvement, mentorship, and local area commitment.

Bank of America's victory lies in its obligation to making a working environment where each person, paying little mind to foundation, can flourish. The organization effectively upholds worker organizations, mentorship projects, and drives that advance inclusivity. By focusing on variety and consideration, Bank of America has drawn in top ability as well as developed a culture that esteems the novel commitments of every worker.

Groundbreaking Effect of Comprehensive Recruiting Practices

Taking everything into account, the examples of overcoming adversity of organizations embracing comprehensive recruiting rehearses feature the groundbreaking effect of variety and incorporation on authoritative achievement. Whether through orientation equity drives, neurodiversity projects, or thorough variety and consideration techniques, these organizations have shown that cultivating a different and comprehensive labor force isn't just an ethical objective yet additionally a competitive edge.

The victories of these organizations go past mathematical portrayal; they stretch out to making work environment societies where each individual feels esteemed, upheld, and engaged to contribute their extraordinary points of view and gifts. As these examples of overcoming adversity keep on motivating, they make ready for a future where comprehensive employing rehearses are a pattern as well as a principal part of hierarchical greatness, driving development, and making positive social effect.

8.3 Creating an autism-friendly workplace culture.

Making a Mental imbalance Accommodating Work environment Culture: Cultivating Incorporation, Understanding, and Strengthening

In the journey for variety and consideration, organizations are progressively perceiving the significance of making a chemical imbalance accommodating working environment culture. This story investigates the multi-layered methodologies and drives that associations can take on to cultivate a climate where people on the mental imbalance range feel acknowledged as well as enabled to flourish in their expert undertakings.

Building Mindfulness and Understanding

A basic move toward making a mental imbalance accommodating working environment culture is building mindfulness and understanding among representatives. Numerous confusions and generalizations encompass chemical imbalance, and encouraging a comprehensive climate starts with scattering these fantasies. Organizations can sort out mindfulness meetings, studios, and preparing projects to teach workers about the assorted idea of the chemical imbalance range.

The victory of building mindfulness lies in the formation of a work environment where partners get it and value the one of a kind qualities and difficulties of their neurodivergent peers. By developing compassion and dispersing generalizations, associations can make an establishment for a strong culture where people on the mental imbalance range feel seen, heard, and comprehended.

Carrying out Tangible Cordial Plan

Tangible responsiveness is a typical quality among people on the mental imbalance range, and organizations can find proactive ways to make a tactile well disposed work environment. This includes considering elements, for example, lighting, clamor levels, and work area plan to oblige different tangible necessities.

Straightforward changes, for example, giving sound blocking earphones or making calm spaces, can essentially add to a more comprehensive climate.

The victory of tangible amicable plan is apparent in the expanded solace and efficiency of representatives on the chemical imbalance range. By perceiving and tending to tactile responsive qualities, associations exhibit a guarantee to making a work area that esteems the different requirements, everything being equal, cultivating a culture of incorporation and understanding.

Adaptable Work Game plans and Facilities

Adaptability in work game plans is a critical component in making a mental imbalance accommodating work environment. Perceiving that people on the chemical imbalance range might flourish in various workplaces or expect changes in accordance with their schedules, organizations can offer adaptable timetables, remote work choices, and modified facilities.

The victory of adaptable work game plans lies in giving neurodivergent representatives the independence to structure their work such that suits their singular requirements. Whether it includes adaptable hours, remote work potential open doors, or explicit work environment facilities, associations that focus on adaptability add to the prosperity and progress of their neurodivergent labor force.

Advancing Comprehensive Correspondence Practices

Correspondence is a foundation of any work environment culture, and embracing comprehensive correspondence rehearses is fundamental for establishing a chemical imbalance accommodating climate. Clear and direct correspondence, visual guides, and composed guidelines can upgrade understanding for people on the mental imbalance range. Organizations can likewise give correspondence preparing to all workers to advance a culture of viable and comprehensive collaboration.

The victory of comprehensive correspondence lies in the making of a work environment where all people, paying little heed to neurodiversity, can successfully comprehend and pass on data. By encouraging a climate where various correspondence styles are perceived and obliged, associations add to a culture of coordinated effort and common regard.

Laying out Mentorship and Backing Projects

Mentorship and backing programs assume a critical part in assisting people on the chemical imbalance range with coordinating into the working environment effectively. Matching neurodivergent workers with tutors who comprehend their one of a kind requirements can give important direction and backing. These projects can likewise incorporate companion encouraging groups of people, making a feeling of local area and fellowship.

The victory of mentorship and backing programs is clear in the expert development and certainty of neurodivergent representatives. By laying out associations and offering a help framework, associations add to the comprehensive prosperity of their neurodivergent labor force, cultivating a climate where everybody can arrive at their maximum capacity.

Offering Preparing for Directors and Representatives

Preparing programs for the two directors and representatives are fundamental parts of making a mental imbalance accommodating work environment culture. Directors can profit from preparing that outfits them with the information and abilities to help neurodivergent colleagues successfully. Likewise, preparing for all workers helps construct a culture of figuring out, sympathy, and acknowledgment.

The victory of preparing programs lies in the production of a learned and strong labor force. By giving the devices to supervisors and partners to comprehend and explore the exceptional parts of working with people on the chemical imbalance range, associations add to a culture where variety isn't just recognized yet celebrated.

Observing Neurodiversity Through Representative Asset Gatherings (ERGs)

Representative Asset Gatherings (ERGs) committed to neurodiversity can act as strong promoters for making a comprehensive working environment culture. These gatherings give a stage to neurodivergent workers to share encounters, offer bits of knowledge, and team up on drives that advance getting it and acknowledgment.

The victory of neurodiversity ERGs lies in their capacity to make a feeling of local area and having a place. By cultivating associations and empowering open exchange, these gatherings add to the more extensive social shift towards perceiving and commending neurodiversity as an indispensable piece of the authoritative personality.

Giving Profession Advancement Open doors

Making a mental imbalance accommodating working environment culture includes giving equivalent chances to vocation improvement and progression. Organizations can execute drives that emphasis on the abilities and qualities of neurodivergent people, giving custom fitted profession ways and potential learning experiences.

The victory of vocation improvement drives is apparent in the expert achievement and fulfillment of neurodivergent representatives. By perceiving and sustaining ability, associations add to a culture where variety isn't recently recognized yet effectively coordinated into the texture of profession movement and achievement.

Estimating and Evaluating Inclusivity

Routinely estimating and evaluating the inclusivity of work environment rehearses is fundamental for making a mental imbalance accommodating society. This includes gathering criticism from neurodivergent representatives, checking the outcome of executed drives, and making changes in view of the developing requirements of the labor force.

The victory of estimation lies in the association's obligation to persistent improvement. By routinely evaluating inclusivity measurements and effectively looking for input, organizations exhibit a commitment to establishing a climate where people on the mental imbalance range can flourish, adding to a work environment culture that develops with the different necessities of its representatives.

Encouraging a Culture of Strengthening and Promotion

At last, the victory of making a chemical imbalance accommodating working environment culture lies in encouraging a culture of strengthening and support. Associations can enable neurodivergent workers by giving them the devices, assets, and backing expected to succeed in their jobs. Backing includes effectively advancing neurodiversity both inside and outside the association, adding to more extensive cultural change.

The victory of strengthening and backing is apparent in the expanded certainty, work fulfillment, and in general prosperity of neurodivergent representatives. By cultivating a culture where people on the chemical imbalance range are obliged as well as effectively engaged to contribute, associations set a trend for inclusivity and make ready for a more different and tolerating proficient scene.

Extraordinary Effect of a Chemical imbalance Accommodating Work environment

All in all, the making of a mental imbalance accommodating work environment culture is an extraordinary excursion that goes past simple convenience — it includes effectively encouraging a culture where neurodivergent people can flourish, contribute, and feel esteemed. The victories inside every technique and drive add to a more extensive story of inclusivity, understanding, and acknowledgment inside the hierarchical system.

As organizations progressively perceive the advantages of neurodiversity, the excursion towards a mental imbalance accommodating working environment becomes a demonstration of hierarchical greatness as well as an impression of cultural advancement. The effect of making such a culture stretches out past the working environment, impacting perspectives, destroying generalizations, and encouraging an existence where people on the mental imbalance range are commended for their extraordinary commitments.

Chapter 9

Community Connections

Local area Associations: The Force of Building More grounded Ties

In the complex embroidered artwork of human life, local area associations arise as crucial strings that wind around together the structure holding the system together. The idea of local area rises above topographical limits and includes shared interests, values, and a feeling of having a place. This account investigates the multi-layered elements of local area associations, digging into their importance, the bonds they make, and the groundbreaking effect they have on people and society at large.

The Substance of Local area: Past Geological Nearness

Local area, in its most genuine sense, reaches out a long ways past the customary bounds of topographical vicinity. It encapsulates shared encounters, shared objectives, and a feeling of aggregate personality that joins people regardless of actual distances. Whether conformed to an area, a social gathering, or a common interest, networks act as central mainstays of human association.

The victory of local area lies in its capacity to connect holes, cultivate understanding, and give a feeling of safety and backing. Networks go about as microcosms where people can communicate their true selves, share their accounts, and track down comfort in the shared traits that predicament them. In an undeniably interconnected world, the idea of local area develops, embracing virtual spaces, online gatherings, and worldwide organizations that resist the constraints of actual limits.

Building Bonds: Shared Interests and Normal Qualities

At the core of vigorous local area associations are shared interests and normal qualities that make a feeling of union and brotherhood. Whether based on leisure activities, callings, or backing, networks structure naturally as people with comparable interests meet up. These common pursuits act as the structure blocks for bonds that rise above superficial cooperations, cultivating a more profound feeling of association.

The victory of shared interests lies in the production of spaces where people can track down close companions, trade thoughts, and work together towards normal goals. Whether it's a book club examining writing, an avid supporter local area commending triumphs and losses, or a web-based gathering joining people with specialty interests, these networks give a feeling of having a place and approval. Through shared encounters, local area individuals produce enduring associations that add to their self-improvement and satisfaction.

Social and Variety People group: Observing Uniqueness

Networks additionally arise around shared social foundations and praise the wealth of variety inside society. Social people group give a space to people to interface with their legacy, customs, and dialects, cultivating a feeling of satisfaction and having a place. These people group assume a urgent part in saving and advancing social variety, guaranteeing that extraordinary practices are passed down from one age to another.

The victory of social and variety networks lies in their capacity to separate generalizations, advance comprehension, and make comprehensive spaces where people from different foundations can coincide agreeably. These people group become stages for social trade, where individuals commend their own legacy as well as gain bits of knowledge into the extravagance of others'. Through this trade, biases are destroyed, and an embroidery of shared humankind is woven, reinforcing the bonds that interface every one of us.

Emotionally supportive networks: Sustaining Emotional well-being and Prosperity

In the midst of win and difficulty, networks act as significant emotionally supportive networks, giving close to home, mental, and reasonable help. Whether confronting individual difficulties, praising accomplishments, or exploring life's vulnerabilities, people inside a local area track down comfort in realizing that they are in good company. The securities fashioned inside these networks make a well-being net that advances psychological well-being and prosperity.

The victory of emotionally supportive networks inside networks is apparent in the flexibility they impart in people. Be it a very close family, a circles, or a web-based help bunch, these networks offer a space for people to share weaknesses, look for direction, and get sympathy. Through aggregate strength, local area associations become a wellspring of fortitude and strengthening, assisting people with exploring the intricacies of existence with a feeling of mutual perspective.

Local area Effect on Society: Driving Change and Progress

Networks, when joined by a common vision, have the ability to drive massive change and progress inside society. From grassroots developments upholding for civil rights to nearby drives tending to ecological worries, the aggregate activity of networks can possibly shape the course of history. The victory of local area influence lies in its capacity to prepare people towards a shared objective, affecting positive change on both miniature and large scale scales.

Networks become impetuses for social change by bringing issues to light, coordinating efforts, and utilizing the aggregate strength of their individuals. The securities framed inside these networks intensify individual voices, changing them into a reverberating chorale that requests consideration and activity. Through promotion, schooling, and grassroots endeavors, networks add to making an all the more, evenhanded, and reasonable world.

Difficulties and Flexibility: Exploring the Intricacies

While people group give a heap of advantages, they are not resistant to challenges. Conflicts, clashes, and inside elements can test the versatility of local area associations. In any case, the victory lies in the capacity of networks to explore these intricacies, gain from difficulties, and arise more grounded.

Tough people group effectively take part in open correspondence, compromise, and encouraging a comprehensive climate where various points of view are recognized and regarded. By tending to difficulties head-on, networks exhibit their ability for development and variation. The common obligation to beating snags turns into a binding together power, building up the securities that keep the local area intact.

Innovation and Virtual People group: Reclassifying Association

In the computerized age, innovation assumes a urgent part in reclassifying the scene of local area associations. Virtual people group, worked with by online stages and web-based entertainment, rise above geological boundaries and empower people with shared interests to interface across the globe. The victory of innovation lies in its ability to democratize admittance to local area, making it workable for similar people to view as one another paying little heed to actual distance.

Virtual people group unite people who might not have the amazing chance to associate in conventional settings. Whether it's a web-based help bunch for a particular medical issue, a worldwide organization of experts in a specialty industry, or a virtual book club interfacing perusers around the world, innovation grows the opportunities for local area building. In any case, it additionally presents new elements and difficulties, like the requirement for advanced proficiency, overseeing on the web behavior, and resolving issues connected with cyberbullying or deception.

The Persevering through Tradition of Local area Associations

All, locally associations stand as a demonstration of the getting through tradition of human relationship and shared encounters. Whether established in actual areas or flourishing in the advanced domain, networks act as impetuses for social union, self-improvement, and aggregate advancement. The victory of local area associations lies in their capacity to rise above contrasts, offer help, and make spaces where people can truly communicate their thoughts.

As society keeps on advancing, the job of networks stays vital to the human experience. The woven artwork of associations we wind through shared interests, values, and emotionally supportive networks adds to the lavishness of our aggregate story. By perceiving the force of local area associations, encouraging inclusivity, and embracing the different strings that contain the structure holding the system together, we can keep on building an existence where the victory of local area lies in the strength of our interconnectedness.

9.1 The importance of community support for individuals on the spectrum.

The Significance of Local area Backing for People on the Mental imbalance Range: Sustaining Consideration, Understanding, and Prosperity

In the many-sided scene of neurodiversity, people on the mental imbalance range track down significant importance in the hug of steady networks.

The excursion of exploring the remarkable difficulties and commending the victories of neurodivergent people is intrinsically entwined with the strength and grasping encouraged inside these networks. This story investigates the complex significance of local area support for people on the mental imbalance range, diving into the extraordinary effect on their lives and the more extensive cultural scene.

Cultivating Consideration and Acknowledgment

At the center of local area support for people on the mental imbalance range lies the groundbreaking force of incorporation and acknowledgment. In a world that may not necessarily in every case take special care of the different necessities and points of view of neurodivergent people, networks act as safe-havens where acknowledgment isn't just energized yet celebrated. The victory of cultivating consideration is apparent in the making of spaces where people on the chemical imbalance range feel esteemed for their novel commitments.

Comprehensive people group become stages for separating obstructions and dissipating legends encompassing chemical imbalance. By encouraging a climate that perceives and embraces neurodiversity, these networks add to moving cultural perspectives. The comprehension developed inside these strong spaces rises above simple resistance; it develops into a festival of the different manners by which people on the chemical imbalance range insight and draw in with the world.

Making Encouraging groups of people

Local area support gives the establishment to vigorous and strong encouraging groups of people that become life savers for people on the chemical imbalance range and their families. The victory of these encouraging groups of people lies in the feeling of association, shared encounters, and the consolation that comes from realizing that others have confronted comparative difficulties. Whether in-person help gatherings, online discussions, or local area associations, these organizations become priceless assets for data, direction, and everyday reassurance.

Encouraging groups of people frequently reach out past people with chemical imbalance to incorporate their families, parental figures, and partners. This all encompassing methodology recognizes the interconnectedness of the difficulties looked by the whole emotionally supportive network. The common excursion inside these organizations adds to an aggregate victory over misfortune, encouraging a feeling of solidarity and shared understanding.

Tending to Disgrace and Support

Local area support assumes a crucial part in tending to the shame related with chemical imbalance range conditions. Shame emerges from confusions, generalizations, and an absence of grasping about neurodiversity. Strong people group become advocates, testing these misguided judgments and effectively advancing mindfulness and instruction. The victory of backing lies in the slow destroying of cultural obstructions and the advancement of a comprehensive account that perceives the qualities and capacities of people on the chemical imbalance range.

Through coordinated backing endeavors, networks enhance the voices of neurodivergent people and their partners. These endeavors might appear as mindfulness crusades, instructive drives, or official support. By effectively taking part in forming public talk, steady networks add to the formation of a more comprehensive and compassionate society that esteems the extraordinary commitments of every one of its individuals.

Exploring Instructive Difficulties

For people on the chemical imbalance range, the instructive excursion can introduce novel difficulties that reach out past conventional scholarly obstacles. Steady people group become essential partners in exploring these difficulties, whether in standard instructive settings or particular projects. The victory of local area support in training is apparent in the production of conditions that oblige different learning styles and give the vital assets to scholarly achievement.

Comprehensive instructive networks perceive the significance of customized approaches that consider the tactile responsive qualities, correspondence styles, and individualized needs of neurodivergent understudies. These people group advocate for comprehensive instruction rehearses, instructor preparing, and the execution of help administrations to guarantee that instructive spaces are inviting and obliging for people on the chemical imbalance range.

Advancing Work Open doors

Local area support broadens its venture into the domain of business, where people on the chemical imbalance range frequently face explicit difficulties connected with social collaborations, tactile awarenesses, and correspondence. Strong people group assume a critical part in advancing comprehensive business open doors, encouraging work environment conditions that esteem neurodiversity. The victory here isn't simply in getting position situations however in making working environments that perceive and use the exceptional qualities of neurodivergent people.

Networks might team up with bosses to carry out neurodiversity recruiting drives, give working environment facilities, and proposition mentorship programs. By pushing for comprehensive business rehearses, these networks add to destroying boundaries to proficient achievement and advancing the significant consideration of people on the chemical imbalance range in the labor force.

Supporting Interactive abilities and Connections

One of the victories of local area support for people on the chemical imbalance range is the sustaining of interactive abilities and the help of significant connections. Social connections can be perplexing for neurodivergent people, and steady networks become research centers for the turn of events and practice of interactive abilities. Whether through coordinated get-togethers, peer support gatherings, or mentorship programs, these networks give places of refuge to people to assemble associations and fellowships.

Comprehensive social networks perceive the variety of social inclinations and correspondence styles inside the neurodivergent local area. They cultivate a climate where people can communicate their thoughts legitimately, gain from each other, and foster the relational abilities vital for exploring social scenes. The victory isn't just in that frame of mind of interactive abilities however in the development of a feeling of having a place and brotherhood.

Enabling Self-Promotion

Local area support enables people on the chemical imbalance range to become self-advocates, stating their privileges, communicating their requirements, and adding to choices that influence their lives. The victory of self-backing lies in the shift from being uninvolved beneficiaries of help to dynamic members in molding their own fates. Strong people group give the information, apparatuses, and stages for people to explain their encounters and supporter for foundational changes that advance inclusivity.

Self-promotion reaches out to different aspects of life, including training, business, medical services, and local area investment. People on the mental imbalance range, fully backed by steady networks, can take part in support endeavors that challenge generalizations, advance comprehension, and establish conditions where their voices are heard as well as esteemed.

Upgrading Personal satisfaction

Eventually, the general victory of local area support for people on the mental imbalance range is the upgrade of their general personal satisfaction. Strong people group add to a comprehensive methodology that tends to the complex parts of prosperity, incorporating actual wellbeing, emotional well-being, social associations, and individual satisfaction. The significance of local area support is reflected in the unmistakable enhancements in the existences of neurodivergent people and their families.

Steady people group might team up with medical services suppliers, advisors, and social administrations to guarantee thorough and individualized care. This cooperative methodology adds to separating hindrances to getting to important administrations and encourages a climate where neurodivergent people can lead satisfying lives, seek after their inclinations, and contribute seriously to their networks.

Determination: An Aggregate Victory

All in all, the significance of local area support for people on the mental imbalance range is a story of aggregate victory — a victory over confinement, shame, and fundamental hindrances. Strong people group become guides of grasping, acknowledgment, and strengthening. The extraordinary effect of these networks stretches out past individual lives, molding the more extensive cultural scene and adding to a world that values neurodiversity as an intrinsic and important part of humankind.

The victories inside these networks are secluded minutes as well as nonstop accounts of versatility, backing, and incorporation. As society progressively perceives the significance of encouraging steady networks, the victory turns into a common excursion — one where the strength of aggregate comprehension makes ready for a more humane, comprehensive, and impartial future for people on the mental imbalance range.

9.2 Grassroots initiatives promoting inclusivity.

Grassroots Drives Advancing Inclusivity: Supporting Change From the beginning

In the steadily advancing embroidered artwork of cultural advancement, grassroots drives arise as strong impetuses for change, especially in the domain of inclusivity. These drives, established in nearby networks and driven by enthusiastic people, make light of a groundbreaking job in breaking boundaries, testing standards, and it isn't simply recognized yet celebrated to encourage conditions where variety. This account investigates the complex scene of grassroots drives advancing inclusivity, digging into their importance, wins, and the more extensive effect they have on forming more fair and inviting social orders.

The Groundwork of Grassroots Drives: Neighborhood Strengthening

At the core of grassroots drives advancing inclusivity is the idea of neighborhood strengthening. These drives start naturally from inside networks, driven by people who are personally associated with the difficulties and potential open doors present in their neighborhood settings.

The victory of grassroots endeavors lies in their capacity to address explicit necessities, connect straightforwardly with local area individuals, and influence neighborhood information to make enduring change.

Neighborhood strengthening cultivates a feeling of responsibility and organization among local area individuals, changing them from uninvolved beneficiaries of progress to dynamic patrons. Whether resolving issues of racial imbalance, LGBTQ+ freedoms, or availability for people with handicaps, grassroots drives exemplify the rule that significant change frequently begins at the local area level.

Making Spaces for Discourse and Understanding

Grassroots drives act as essential stages for encouraging discourse and understanding inside networks. Inclusivity, at its center, requires transparent discussions about contrasts, inclinations, and the foundational boundaries that exist. The victory of grassroots drives in such manner is clear in their capacity to make places of refuge where different viewpoints are invited as well as effectively looked for.

These drives work with discussions that challenge assumptions, destroy generalizations, and advance compassion. Whether through local area gatherings, narrating occasions, or studios, grassroots coordinators set out open doors for people to share their encounters, cultivating an aggregate comprehension that is fundamental for building comprehensive networks.

Tending to Multifacetedness and Various Viewpoints

One of the victories of grassroots drives advancing inclusivity is their acknowledgment of multifacetedness and the significance of embracing assorted viewpoints. Inclusivity goes past recognizing contrasts in confinement; it requires a comprehension of how different parts of character converge and shape individual encounters. Grassroots endeavors, frequently started by people with lived encounters, effectively pursue tending to the intricacies of interconnection.

Drives that attention on the diversity of race, orientation, sexuality, and different characters make more nuanced and extensive ways to deal with inclusivity. The victory lies in the affirmation that people might explore various layers of character, and advancing inclusivity requires tending to the interconnected difficulties and honors related with these personalities.

Instructive Effort and Mindfulness Missions

Grassroots drives assume a crucial part in instructive effort and mindfulness crusades that challenge generalizations and advance a more comprehensive story. Instruction is an integral asset for destroying biases and encouraging a culture of understanding. The victory of grassroots instructive drives lies in their capacity to connect straightforwardly with local area individuals, giving data, assets, and encouraging decisive reasoning.

These drives might appear as studios in schools, local area drove workshops, or online missions intended to contact a more extensive crowd. Grassroots coordinators perceive the effect of scattering legends and falsehood, effectively adding to a more educated and mindful local area that is better prepared to embrace variety.

Pushing for Strategy Changes

While grassroots drives frequently start at the local area level, their effect much of the time stretches out to pushing for more extensive arrangement changes. The victory of these drives isn't bound to confined upgrades yet frequently brings about foundational shifts that have expansive results. Grassroots coordinators, powered by the longing for inclusivity, become advocates for strategy changes that address underlying disparities and advance equivalent open doors.

Whether pushing for hostile to separation regulations, openness principles, or instructive strategies that focus on inclusivity, grassroots drives add to the production of a more fair legitimate and social system. The outcome of these endeavors is clear in the regulative changes that mirror a pledge to encouraging inclusivity for a bigger scope.

Cultivating Financial Inclusivity and Business venture

Grassroots drives advancing inclusivity broaden their effect into the financial domain by cultivating business venture and monetary inclusivity. Enabling underestimated networks monetarily is a victory that goes past foundation; it includes setting out feasible open doors that permit people to contribute effectively to their nearby economies. Grassroots drives frequently focus on drives, for example, local area based organizations, ability improvement projects, and mentorship open doors.

The victory of monetary inclusivity lies in separating boundaries to section and making pathways for people from different foundations to flourish. Grassroots coordinators make progress toward evening the odds, perceiving that monetary strengthening is a vital part of generally inclusivity that upgrades the prosperity of networks.

Building Strong Organizations for Underestimated Gatherings

One of the center victories of grassroots drives advancing inclusivity is the making of strong organizations for minimized gatherings. Whether zeroing in on LGBTQ+ privileges, racial equity, or handicap promotion, these drives effectively make progress toward destroying foundational boundaries and giving a feeling of local area and having a place for the people who might feel minimized. Grassroots endeavors perceive the significance of portrayal and effectively look to intensify the voices of the individuals who have generally been underrepresented.

Steady organizations made by grassroots drives become wellsprings of solidarity, versatility, and strengthening. They act as spaces where people can share assets, encounters, and backing each other in exploring the difficulties related with their personalities. The victory is clear in the making of networks that promoter for change as well as effectively elevate and engage their individuals.

Ecological Inclusivity: Associating Individuals and Nature

Grassroots drives advancing inclusivity stretch out their compass to ecological inclusivity, perceiving the interconnectedness among individuals and the regular world. Natural equity drives frequently emerge from nearby networks that endure the worst part of ecological imbalances. The victory of these grassroots endeavors is twofold: they address natural issues that excessively influence minimized networks, and they make spaces for assorted voices to be heard in conversations about maintainability and protection.

These drives might include local area gardens, preservation activities, or promotion for manageable metropolitan preparation. Grassroots coordinators perceive that ecological inclusivity goes past protection; it includes guaranteeing that all networks approach clean air, water, and green spaces, paying little heed to financial status.

Difficulties and Versatility: The Coarseness of Grassroots Drives

While grassroots drives advancing inclusivity accomplish outstanding victories, they are not without challenges. Restricted assets, institutional obstruction, and burnout are normal obstacles looked by grassroots coordinators. Nonetheless, the strength of these drives lies in their flexibility and grassroots coordinators' obligation to their causes. Defeating difficulties turns out to be essential for the account, exhibiting the coarseness and assurance of those devoted to cultivating inclusivity starting from the earliest stage.

Grassroots drives frequently answer difficulties with inventiveness, coordinated effort, and a profound comprehension of the networks they serve. The capacity to turn and adjust methodologies despite difficulty is a demonstration of the grassroots methodology's deftness and viability in tending to the consistently developing elements of inclusivity.

Computerized Stages and Worldwide Effect

In the computerized age, grassroots drives elevating inclusivity influence innovation to enhance their effect and contact worldwide crowds. Online stages and virtual entertainment become integral assets for associating similar people, sharing assets, and preparing support. The victory of computerized grassroots drives is obvious in their capacity to rise above geological limits, considering the trading of thoughts and systems on a worldwide scale.

Computerized stages give a space to underestimated voices to be heard, and online activism turns into a strong power for change. Grassroots coordinators can use innovation to sort out virtual occasions, direct internet based mindfulness missions, and assemble networks that reach out a long ways past the limits of neighborhood networks. The worldwide effect of these drives adds to a more extensive discussion about inclusivity that rises above social and local limits.

An Embroidery Woven with Variety and Consideration

All in all, grassroots drives advancing inclusivity weave an embroidery of progress that celebrates variety, challenges disparities, and encourages conditions where everybody feels seen, heard, and esteemed. The victory of these drives lies not just in the restricted upgrades they achieve yet in the more extensive social shift towards a more comprehensive and fair society.

As grassroots coordinators keep on supporting inclusivity, their effect turns into an essential piece of the aggregate story of progress. The flexibility, innovativeness, and enduring responsibility showed by those driving grassroots drives embody the extraordinary force of local area driven change. In our current reality where inclusivity isn't simply an objective yet a common obligation, grassroots endeavors stand as encouraging signs, enlightening the way towards an all the more, empathetic, and comprehensive future for all.

9.3 Building bridges between the autism community and society at large.

Building Scaffolds Between the Chemical imbalance Local area and Society at Large: Fostering Getting it, Inclusivity, and Compassion

In the complicated embroidery of human variety, the chemical imbalance local area remains as a dynamic and essential string, winding around one of a kind stories, viewpoints, and qualities into the more extensive cultural texture. The excursion toward building spans between the mental imbalance local area and society in general is a story of figuring out, inclusivity, and sympathy. This investigation dives into the complex elements of this extension building process, inspecting the difficulties, wins, and the groundbreaking effect on both the chemical imbalance local area and the more extensive social scene.

The Range's Variety: Perceiving Individual Stories

At the center of building spans is the acknowledgment of the assorted and individualized nature of the mental imbalance range. The mental imbalance local area envelops a range of encounters, qualities, and difficulties, opposing a one-size-fits-all methodology. Building understanding requires an affirmation that every person on the range explores an interesting excursion molded by variables, for example, tangible responsive qualities, correspondence styles, and co-happening conditions.

The victory in perceiving this variety lies in dispersing generalizations and misguided judgments. By embracing the lavishness of individual accounts inside the chemical imbalance local area, society ventures out toward building spans established on certifiable comprehension and acknowledgment. It turns into an excursion of esteeming neurodiversity as an innate part of the human experience.

Schooling and Mindfulness: Enlightening the Way to Understanding

Building spans requires enlightening the way to figuring out through instruction and mindfulness. Numerous misguided judgments encompassing mental imbalance originate from an absence of data and openness. Win in this domain is accomplished through drives that bring issues to light, scatter exact data, and

cultivate a culture of consistent learning. Instructive missions, studios, and local area occasions become urgent in exposing fantasies and giving bits of knowledge into the assorted ways people on the mental imbalance range experience the world.

The victory is obvious when society at large becomes educated about the qualities, difficulties, and subtleties of mental imbalance. As understanding develops, assumptions are supplanted with information, and the scaffold between the mental imbalance local area and the more extensive society is strengthened with the solid mainstays of compassion and mindfulness.

Cultivating Comprehensive Spaces: From Attention to Activity

Mindfulness, in any case, is only the start. The genuine victory lies in making an interpretation of mindfulness right into it by encouraging comprehensive spaces that oblige the necessities of people on the mental imbalance range. Comprehensive plan standards stretch out past actual spaces to incorporate instructive organizations, work environments, sporting facilities, and social conditions.

Making tangible well disposed spaces, executing comprehensive instruction rehearses, and laying out neurodiverse-accommodating work environments embody the victory of inclusivity. At the point when people on the chemical imbalance range can explore and partake in different parts of existence without unnecessary obstructions, the scaffold turns into a two-way lane, considering the consistent joining of assorted encounters into the more extensive cultural scene.

Paying attention to Lived Encounters: Hoisting Voices Inside the Local area

Building spans includes tuning in as well as effectively raising the voices of people inside the chemical imbalance local area. Win in this setting is accomplished when those with lived encounters are given stages to share their accounts, experiences, and points of view. Their stories become amazing assets for destroying generalizations and encouraging a more profound comprehension of the variety inside the mental imbalance range.

Through drives, for example, narrating occasions, backing efforts drove by people on the range, and the advancement of self-promotion, society starts to perceive the ability that comes from lived encounters. This height of voices makes a scaffold based on shared regard, where the chemical imbalance local area isn't just heard however effectively engaged with forming the stories that characterize their encounters.

Encouraging groups of people and Strengthening: Reinforcing the Establishment

Building spans requires a strong groundwork of encouraging groups of people and strengthening systems. Win in this perspective is seen when families, parental figures, and partners effectively take part in making a strong environment. Local area associations, support gatherings, and online organizations become channels for sharing assets, looking for guidance, and cultivating a feeling of having a place.

The victory isn't simply in that frame of mind of these organizations however in their adequacy in giving functional help and everyday encouragement. At the point when families and people on the mental imbalance range feel engaged to explore difficulties, the scaffold between the local area and society at large becomes a help of shared strength and versatility.

Joint effort Across Areas: Separating Storehouses

The victory of building spans is amplified when joint effort rises above sectoral limits. Joint effort across schooling, medical care, business, and social administrations becomes instrumental in making a comprehensive emotionally supportive network. This cooperative methodology guarantees that people on the chemical imbalance range get extensive consideration and open doors that length different parts of their lives.

Separating storehouses includes cultivating correspondence and coordination among assorted partners, including instructors, medical services experts, managers, policymakers, and local area advocates. At the point when these areas team up, the extension turns into a very much associated network, supporting that inclusivity is an aggregate liability that stretches out past separated endeavors.

Media Portrayal: Molding Positive Stories

The media assumes a urgent part in molding public discernments and stories. Win in building spans happens when media portrayal of people on the mental imbalance range moves past drama or generalizations. Positive and genuine depictions in films, TV, writing, and different types of media add to adjusting cultural mentalities.

The victory lies in the development of a story that features the qualities, accomplishments, and regular encounters of people on the chemical imbalance range. At the point when media portrayal turns into an impression of the variety inside the local area, it supports the extension as a conductor for exact seeing instead of sustaining hurtful generalizations.

Strategy Support: Changing Foundational Approaches

Building spans additionally includes supporting for strategy changes that change fundamental ways to deal with mental imbalance. The victory in approach support is seen when authoritative structures focus on inclusivity, openness, and equivalent open doors for people on the mental imbalance range. This incorporates arrangements connected with instruction, work, medical care, and social administrations.

Powerful arrangements are those that effectively address the exceptional necessities of the mental imbalance local area, guaranteeing that lawful structures line up with the standards of neurodiversity. Win is estimated in the unmistakable effect of approaches that destroy fundamental hindrances and establish a climate where people on the chemical imbalance range can flourish and contribute seriously.

Local area Commitment: A Common Obligation

The scaffold building process is a common obligation that includes dynamic local area commitment. Win is accomplished when networks effectively take part in drives that advance inclusivity, whether through volunteerism, local area occasions, or neighborhood support endeavors. At the point when inclusivity becomes implanted in the shared mindset of networks, the scaffold turns into an impression of shared values and a promise to encouraging a different and inviting society.

Local area commitment additionally includes making spaces for discourse, where people from varying backgrounds can meet up to learn, share, and celebrate variety.

These discoursed add to the fortifying of the extension, cultivating associations in light of common regard, compassion, and a common obligation to inclusivity.

Training for Sympathy: Supporting People in the future

Building spans is an intergenerational attempt, and win lies in sustaining compassion and understanding among people in the future. Instructive educational programs that integrate examples on neurodiversity, sympathy building exercises, and comprehensive study hall rehearses add to forming a more caring and tolerating society.

At the point when youthful personalities are presented to the standards of inclusivity since the beginning, the scaffold building process becomes imbued in cultural qualities. Instruction for compassion guarantees that people in the future not just perceive the variety inside the chemical imbalance local area however effectively add to making a reality where everybody is embraced for what their identity is.

An Extension That Develops Further with Time

All in all, building spans between the chemical imbalance local area and society in general is a dynamic and progressing process set apart by ceaseless development and understanding. The victories along this excursion are not separated occasions but rather an aggregate story of progress, versatility, and a common obligation to inclusivity.

The scaffold that associates the mental imbalance local area and society in general isn't static; it develops with each demonstration of grasping, every drive for inclusivity, and every snapshot of sympathy. The genuine victory lies in the development of the scaffold as well as in its capacity to endure difficulties, adjust to evolving scenes, and become an image of solidarity in variety. As society keeps on leaving on this excursion, the scaffold turns into a demonstration of the groundbreaking force of cultivating grasping, inclusivity, and sympathy for all.

www.ingramcontent.com/pod-product-compliance
Lightning Source LLC
LaVergne TN
LVHW051303200726
843510LV00010B/1254